GEORGIA
LEGENDS & LORE

ALAN BROWN

THE
History
PRESS

Published by The History Press
Charleston, SC
www.historypress.com

Front cover, top left: by the author. All other cover images from Wikimedia Commons.
All internal images are by the author unless otherwise noted.

First published 2022

Manufactured in the United States

ISBN 9781467151788

Library of Congress Control Number: 2022936627

Notice: The information in this book is true and complete to the best of our knowledge. It is offered without guarantee on the part of the author or The History Press. The author and The History Press disclaim all liability in connection with the use of this book.

CONTENTS

CONTENTS

Contents

INTRODUCTION

The state of Georgia is known for many things. First of all, Georgia is a state rich in history. It was one of the thirteen colonies that rebelled against British rule. Three major Civil War battles were fought in Georgia: Chickamauga, Kennesaw Mountain and Atlanta. Atlanta is also the birthplace of Dr. Martin Luther King Jr., who spearheaded the civil rights movement with the formation of the Southern Christian Leadership Conference (SCLC) in Atlanta in 1957. The state's geography, encompassing mountains, plains and coastal beaches, attracts thousands of visitors annually. Food lovers think of peaches, peanuts and Vidalia onions when the name "Georgia" comes up in conversation. Coca-Cola, one of America's favorite soft drinks, was invented in Atlanta in 1886. Sports fans associate Georgia with the Atlanta Braves, the Atlanta Falcons, the Atlanta Hawks and the Masters at Augusta National Golf Tournament.

However, Georgia also has a dark, mysterious side that has intrigued people for hundreds of years. Stories of lost Civil War gold have lured treasure hunters to Valdosta and Wilkes County for over a century. Legendary killers like John Henry "Doc" Holliday once called Georgia home. Some of the nation's most beautiful—and scariest—cemeteries can be found in Georgia, such as Bonaventure Cemetery (Savannah), St. James Episcopal Cemetery (Marietta) and Oakland Cemetery (Atlanta). Haunted places like the Moon River Brewing Company (Savannah), Calloway Plantation (Washington) and the St. Simon's Lighthouse (St. Simon's Island) are scattered across the state. Georgia women with extraordinary powers, like the "Georgia

Wonder," Lulu Hurst; the "Little Georgia Magnet," Dixie Haygood; and the "Oracle of the Ages," Mayhayley Lancaster, became nationally known. Georgia's UFO sightings received national attention when Governor Jimmy Carter claimed to have seen one in Leary, Georgia. Not only has Georgia had numerous Bigfoot sightings, but a few Georgians have also claimed to see the Talbotton Werewolf and Altamaha-ha, Georgia's sea serpent. Native American legends have been memorialized at Tallulah Gorge (Tallulah Falls) and Stone Pile Gap (Dahlonega). Several of Georgia's colleges and universities are known for their ghost tales, like the University of Georgia (Athens) and Brenau University (Gainesville).

So the next time you are in the mood to get away from reality for a while, fix some peaches and ice cream, munch on some peanuts and enjoy *Georgia Legends & Lore*. If you still need help putting yourself in a Georgia mood, listen to Ray Charles's "Georgia on My Mind."

CIVIL WAR LEGENDS

Andersonville Prison

ANDERSONVILLE

For centuries, prisons throughout the world have been hotbeds of mistreatment and suffering. During the Civil War, however, conditions in Union and Confederate prisons were especially bad. Of the 211,000 Union soldiers incarcerated in Confederate prisons, around 30,000 died. Approximately 26,000 of the 215,000 incarcerated Confederate soldiers perished in Union prisons. Malnutrition and inadequate shelter were commonplace, primarily because most of the officers in charge had no training in prison management. Overcrowding in these prisons worsened after General Ulysses S. Grant canceled all prisoner exchanges in 1864.

Quite possibly the most infamous of all the Civil War prisons was Andersonville. Originally known as Camp Sumter because of its proximity to Sumter County, the twenty-six-acre prison camp was a stockade, enclosed by a high wall constructed of timbers early in 1864. The prison was designed to hold ten thousand prisoners, but by August of that year, thirty-three thousand men were confined in a space 1,620 feet long and 779 feet wide. They lived in tents that gave them little protection from the elements. The swampy area in the middle of the prison only made matters worse. Outbreaks of dysentery claimed hundreds of lives. Latrines and clean

Approximately thirty-three thousand Union soldiers were confined within the stockade walls of Andersonville Prison. *Wikimedia Commons.*

The cemetery resounds with the moans of the restless spirits of the thirteen thousand soldiers who perished at Andersonville Prison. *Wikimedia Commons.*

drinking water were nonexistent. Prisoners who walked across an invisible boundary between the tents and the wall were shot by sentries. Prisoners were also preyed on by sadistic guards and prisoner gangs nicknamed the "Raiders." Because the living conditions at Andersonville Prison were so deplorable, the commanding officer of the prison, Swiss-born Henry Wirz, was hanged for war crimes. Spectators derived a sense of poetic justice from the fact that Wirz's neck was not broken by the hanging; instead, his body dangled helplessly for several minutes until he suffocated.

Because so much suffering and death took place at Andersonville, it would be surprising if the site of the former prison camp had no ghost legends attached to it. People have seen the restless spirit of Henry Wirz walking down the road leading to Andersonville. Some eyewitnesses report seeing Wirz's ghost shaking his head and talking quietly to himself. Cries and moans have been heard by visitors and staff in the prison graveyard. People have also heard whispers, whimpers, yelling and gunfire throughout the site. Some visitors have been overcome by a foul smell wafting through the former prison camp. People have also made out the spectral figures of the prisoners in the fog that rolls across the haunted site. Apparently, for some poor souls, life was so unbearable that they find it impossible to rest in peace, even after death.

BROOKS COUNTY'S BURIED CIVIL WAR TREASURE

VALDOSTA

According to an article posted on the website Valdostatoday.com, soldiers transporting a chest of gold by wagon from South Carolina to Vicksburg buried their cargo near the forks of Okapilco and Mule Creeks in Brooks County. In a variant of the tale, the gold was a large portion of the Confederate treasury that was being hauled from Richmond to Confederate vice president Alexander H. Stephens's relatives in South Georgia following Confederate president Jefferson Davis's capture on May 10, 1865. The story goes that when the wagon train reached the fork of Okapilco and Mule Creeks, a band of either Native Americans or Yankees killed the soldiers guarding the gold and made off with it. Local storytellers cite the Civil War artifacts that have been found in the area—rusted guns, horse bridles, buttons and so on—as proof that this incident really took place. Some locals believe that an iron arrow nailed to an oak tree near the banks of Reedy Creek in Colquitt County indicates where Confederates buried the gold they were transporting.

An entirely different version of Brooks County's buried treasure story dates back to 1750, when fifty Frenchmen were hauling 2,500 pounds of silver from New Orleans to the Gulf Coast. Fearing an attack by unfriendly tribes, the men buried the treasure in Mule Creek Swamp for safekeeping. That night, marauding Native Americans raided their camp, killing the men while they were sleeping. If they knew about the buried silver, the scores of holes that have been dug in the swamp for over two centuries suggest that neither they nor anyone else has found where the cache is buried.

CHICKAMAUGA NATIONAL BATTLEFIELD

CHICKAMAUGA

In June 1863, the Union Army of the Cumberland, under the command of Major General William S. Rosencrans, moved from Murfreesboro, Tennessee, toward Confederate general Braxton Bragg's Army of Tennessee. By late August, Rosencrans's forces had crossed the Tennessee River and advanced southward toward Bragg's railroad supply line. On September 9, Bragg left Chattanooga with reinforcements from Mississippi and East Tennessee. As Rosencrans's army was heading toward Lee and Gordon's Mill on Chickamauga Creek on September 17, Bragg decided to cross the creek southwest toward Lee and Gordon's Mill. The Union forces thwarted Bragg's army several times from crossing the creek. By the time Bragg finally crossed it, he was unable to reach the left flank of the main Union force. On September 18, Rosencrans ordered Major General George H. Thomas to stretch his line from Lee and Gordon's Mill to the Kelly farm. On the morning of September 19, Thomas met fierce resistance from General Nathan Bedford Forrest's cavalry. By the end of the day, the Union army pulled back toward LaFayette Road, where they began constructing breastworks. Late that night, Bragg divided his army into two wings, commanded by Lieutenant General James Longstreet and Lieutenant General Leonidas Polk. Because Polk began his attack several hours late, his troops were driven back. On September 20, Longstreet's wing overwhelmed Wood's troops, forcing them to retreat to Chattanooga. Union general George Henry

Thomas protected the army's rear flank as they were pulling back, earning him the nickname the "Rock of Chickamauga." Technically, the Battle of Chickamauga was a victory for the Confederates because they forced the Union forces to move back to Chattanooga, but it came at a high cost. By the end of the last day, Bragg's army had lost more than eighteen thousand men, while Rosencrans's army lost sixteen thousand men. The Cherokee name for the creek that played such a pivotal role in the battle—Chickamauga, "the river of Death"—proved to be prophetic.

The horrendous carnage at Chickamauga spawned a host of spine-tingling ghost stories. Probably the oldest—and the most famous—ghost legend is the tale of "Old Green Eyes." He is reputed to be the ghost of a Confederate soldier who was decapitated by a cannonball. He crosses the battlefield nightly, searching endlessly for his head. Some folklorists believe that the phantom known as Old Green Eyes can be tracked back to a Native American legend about a ferocious beast that once roamed the area that became Chickamauga Battlefield. The humanoid creature had misshapen jaws with huge, protruding fangs and light-colored fur. Some soldiers and civilians reported seeing this beast prowling among the dead bodies littering the field after the battle.

The story of another headless ghost at Chickamauga Battlefield actually has a basis in fact. Lieutenant Colonel Julius Garesche fell from his horse in the heat of battle and was trampled by the horses running behind him. His body was recovered later, but his head was crushed beneath the pounding hooves of the horses. His spirit is said to be the headless rider that has been sighted galloping through the woods after dark.

A third ghostly sighting is set in the aftermath of the battle, when hordes of women—wives, mothers, sisters and lovers—searched among the dead horses, smashed wagons and cannons and mangled corpses for their loved ones. Some of the more fortunate women found their men in time to nurse them back to health. Those soldiers who died where they fell and were identified were buried in local graveyards. Tragically, the bodies of a large number of the fallen soldiers were never recovered. Approximately 1,500 Confederate soldiers were reported missing in action; approximately 5,000 Federal soldiers remained missing at battle's end. Many of the women continued looking for their men for several days after the last shot was fired. One of these women wandered the battlefield at night, holding a lantern aloft. She was called the Lady in White because of the long white bridal gown she wore as she walked the barren fields along Chickamauga Creek. After she died, the bobbing light of her lantern was a constant sight on

A young man who had climbed Wilder Tower suddenly screamed and jumped off. He was severely injured.

the battlefield after dark. Her apparition, dressed in a fancy, old-fashioned wedding dress, has been sighted primarily in September and October. Eyewitnesses recalled that she was enveloped in an eerie, luminous glow.

At least one of the monuments dotting the battlefield has a ghost story behind it. Built in 1903, Wilder Tower commemorates the courageous stand

People say that the sculpted tiger on top of the Opdycke Monument prowls around the battlefield in a full moon.

of Colonel John T. Wilder's infantry against the Confederate forces. Wilder's men held the enemy off long enough for the Union army to make an orderly retreat. Mementos of the battle were sealed inside the cornerstone of the tower. When the cornerstone was opened in 1976, the contents had mysteriously disappeared. In 1970, an even stranger event took place at the tower. A young man climbed up the tower by holding onto the lightning rod attached to the back of the tower. When he was fourteen feet off the ground, he squeezed into a gun slot and entered the tower. He ran up the steps and called down to his buddies, who were drinking beer. All at once, the boys heard their friend scream inside the tower. He ran down the steps and squeezed through a gun slot that was higher than the one he had originally entered. He plummeted twenty-five feet to the ground, breaking his spine. He survived but never explained what had frightened him so badly inside the Wilder Tower.

Another haunted monument was erected in honor of Opdycke's Tigers, the 125th Ohio Infantry. Emerson Opdycke's soldiers earned fame in their defense of Horseshoe Ridge. The lifelike tiger is said to roam the battlefield on nights when the moon is full.

Fort Pulaski

SAVANNAH

Plans to initiate a coastal system of forts were initiated after the War of 1812. Because the property the federal government had acquired for the fort was marshy, pilings were driven seventy feet under the ground to provide a firm foundation. Construction began in 1830. By the time it was completed in 1847, twenty-five million Savannah Gray and Rose Red bricks had been used to build the five walls. Each wall was seven to eleven feet high. The completed fort consisted of a parade ground, a moat and two powder magazines. By 1861, only twenty guns were in place; therefore, Colonel Charles H. Olmstead's Confederate militia had no trouble taking it over. The Union army's retreat was only temporary, however; for the next several weeks, Federal troops set up thirty-six pieces of heavy artillery on Tybee Island. On April 10, 1862, Union general David Hunter gave the command to begin the bombardment of Fort Pulaski. By April 11, the Union army's rifled cannons had pummeled the fort with 5,275 shells. Later in the afternoon, Colonel Olmstead surrendered Fort Pulaski to General Hunter. Between 1862 and 1863, General Hunter's men repaired the damage to the fort. In 1864, 550 Confederate prisoners were marched into the fort. During their internment at the fort, the soldiers endured malnutrition, dysentery and scurvy; 13 of the prisoners died before the men were transferred to another prion a year later. In 1880, Fort Pulaski was decommissioned, although it was still owned by the War Department. The fort was activated for a brief time during the Spanish-American War before being abandoned. In 1924, the fort was saved by President Calvin Coolidge when he established the Fort Pulaski National Monument. The Department of the Interior acquired the fort on July 28, 1933. Funding from the government enabled the National Park Service to restore, protect and manage the historical site.

Like many Civil War–era masonry forts, Fort Pulaski is reputed to be haunted. Ironically, one of the fort's best-known ghost stories dating back to the Civil War has nothing to do with battles. On November 3, 1863, two teams from New York played baseball inside the fort. The residual sounds of bats hitting balls and the cheering of onlookers echoes through Fort Pulaski at times.

Possibly the most dramatic paranormal occurrence at Fort Pulaski occurred during the filming of *Glory* in 1989. A few scenes of the movie were filmed in Savannah. One day, after filming had stopped, several of the extras decided to visit Fort Pulaski. They were in such a hurry that they did not bother to change out of their Confederate uniforms. The actors had not walked very far into the fort when they were approached by a Confederate soldier wearing an officer's uniform. In an angry voice, he demanded to know why they had not saluted when they passed by him. Before they had a chance to reply, the soldier vanished before their eyes.

The Kennesaw House

MARIETTA

The Marietta Museum is located next to the Marietta Welcome Center and adjacent to the railroad tracks. When the building was constructed in the 1840s, it served as a cotton warehouse. A few years later, the owner converted into a restaurant to accommodate passengers from the nearby railroad depot. In 1855, the next owners of the building, the Fletchers, turned it into an inn. On April 12, 1862, a civilian scout named James J. Andrews hijacked a Confederate locomotive with a band of Union volunteers. They drove the train to Chattanooga, sabotaging the railroad tracks and cutting the telegraph wires along the way before they were captured and executed. In 1864, after the Union army commandeered the inn, General Sherman used it as his headquarters. For a while, the Confederate army used the building as a field hospital. The first major renovation of the building occurred in 1920, when it was converted into retail stores. During the second renovation in 1979, the white façade was removed, revealing the original brickwork underneath. Most of the interior was demolished; in fact, only the wooden staircases and some of the fireplaces are original. The Marietta Museum of History took over the second and third floors of the Kennesaw House in 1996. Exhibits, a gift shop and staff offices were located on the second floor. The third floor was used for storage and additional staff offices. The first floor is now used for event space.

In her book *Haunted Marietta*, author Rhetta Akamatsu wrote about the haunted activity inside the Kennesaw House. Staff members who have taken the elevator to the basement have had a brief vision of bloodstained doctors performing surgeries on screaming soldiers. Other people claim to have been joined on the elevator by a surgeon wearing a Civil War–era

Staff members of the Kennesaw Museum had a fleeting glimpse of a Civil War–era operating table in the basement.

uniform. Children walking through the pink room have seen the ghost of Mrs. Fletcher, whose portrait hangs in the house. In an investigation conducted by the paranormal group Ghost Hounds, the investigators captured the image of a spectral woman on one of their cameras. A different group of paranormal researchers saw the face of a little boy peeking into the hallway.

Another ghostly photo came to the attention of Jan Galt, the director of operations, in 2016. Television station WXIA showed her a photograph of a World War I uniform. On close inspection, the face of a woman could be seen in the photo. Galt insisted that the face in the photo was neither her face nor the face of the woman who was with her. Galt says that the glass on the exhibit was not dirty at the time. She was not surprised by the photograph because of the other reports of haunted activity inside the museum, such as the metallic tapping sounds and the aroma of cigar smoke and popcorn.

KENNESAW MOUNTAIN NATIONAL BATTLEFIELD

KENNESAW

In June 1864, after the Battles of New Hope Church, Pickett's Mill and Dallas, General William Tecumseh Sherman headed east to Acworth, Georgia, to reconnect with his rail supply line. Confederate Joseph Johnston, who had been unable to halt Sherman's advance, formed a new line along the top of Kennesaw Mountain on June 18. During the night, his troops fortified their position by digging trenches and piling up earthworks. Union major general James B. McPherson's Army of the Tennessee soon began a bombardment of Johnston's position on the mountain. On June 21, after moving 11,000 troops from the right to the left of the line, General John Bell Hood was able to stop Sherman's flanking movement. Sherman was reduced to siege tactics until finally attacking the Confederate army on June 27. Sherman's army attempted to soften the Confederate defenses with a withering fire from two hundred guns. Then 5,500 Federal troops moved toward Pigeon Hill. Unfamiliar with the hilly terrain, Sherman's men overran the rifle pits but were unable to penetrate the Confederates' main defenses. After the Union bombardment, Union colonel Daniel McCook's brigade advanced toward Cheatham Hill. His troops managed to cross the wheat field, but when they were within ten or fifteen feet of the Confederate earthworks, the brigade was pummeled with a barrage of bullets. By the end of the barrage, McCook lost all of his field officers and one-third of his men. Still, after brutal hand-to-hand fighting, the Federals dug in at the spot referred to by the Confederate and Union armies as the "Dead Angle." By the end of the day, Sherman's forces suffered 3,000 casualties; the Confederates lost about 1,000 men. This was the end of the fighting at Kennesaw Mountain. Johnston relocated his blockade of the railroad to Atlanta at Smyrna.

Hundreds of visitors to Kennesaw Mountain National Battlefield have reported some sort of paranormal activity. The most common manifestations are the residual sounds of cannon fire and gunfire. Sometimes, the acrid odor of gunpowder and blood wafts across the mountain. Not only have the specters of soldiers been spotted on the battlefield, but so have the ghosts of deer, which have been known to charge people before vanishing. Reenactors have seen wisps of smoke drift over the mountain on the anniversary of the battle.

Approximately three thousand Union soldiers and one thousand Confederate soldiers died in the Battle of Kennesaw Mountain.

One man was walking across the battlefield when he heard someone yelling from the woods. Taking out his phone, the man recorded the strange sounds and played them back. On the recording was a spectral voice saying, "Them soldiers is dead." On the same recording was the sound of distant gunfire.

One of the most publicized sightings at Kennesaw Mountain National Battlefield Park took place in October 2008. A man and his son were driving through the battlefield when, all at once, a man on horseback cut across the road in front of them. The rider appeared to be wearing the uniform of a Union cavalry officer. He was holding his sword aloft. The man jammed on his brakes as the horse rode past his car and proceeded to gallop through a fence. "My son and I were in a state of almost sheer panic, but we managed to maintain and get on the way home very quickly," the man said.

KOLB RIDGE COURT

MARIETTA

On June 19, Major General William Tecumseh Sherman ordered the Army of the Cumberland, commanded by Major General George H. Thomas, to turn the left flank of General Joseph E. Johnston's Army of Tennessee south of Powder Springs Road near Marietta, Georgia. Johnston, in turn, ordered his three corps under Lieutenant General John Bell Hood to move along Powder Springs Road near Mount Zion Church. On the afternoon of June 22, one of Hood's divisions, under the command of Major General Carter L. Stevenson, advanced toward Kolb's Farm south of Powder Springs Road. General Joseph Hooker then moved Major General John W. Geary's division along Powder Springs Road to hold off Hood's attack. When Stevenson's division emerged from the woods north of the woods, Geary's forces forced the Confederates to fall back to a ravine, where they were pummeled by Federal gunfire. The Confederate army lost 1,500 men; Union losses amounted to around 500 soldiers. Sherman's forces may have won the battle, but he was unable to dislodge General Johnston's troops. He then set about preparing for his assault on Kennesaw Mountain on June 27.

Although the Kolb farmhouse and family cemetery remain, much of the battlefield has been lost to development. In their book *Haunted America*, authors Michael Norman and Beth Scott interviewed Katherine and James Tatum, who lived in one of the housing developments on the site of the battlefield. One night, approximately one year after their house was built, James woke up at 2:30 a.m. to use the bedroom bathroom. At the same time, Katherine went to the hall bathroom. As she walked down the hall, she saw a man standing in front of the bathroom door. She assumed that the figure was her husband, so she returned to the bedroom. When she saw James lying in the bed, she realized that a stranger was in the house, so she woke him up. James picked up a gun and searched the house, but no one was there. Katherine tried to go back to sleep, but she kept thinking about the strange man's appearance. She recalled that he was wearing a coat and hat and that he was waving his arms before he vanished at the top of the stairs. All at once, the shocking realization that she had had a brush with something that was not human swept over her.

The Tatums had another eerie experience in the house a month later. James was up in the attic, trying to install a board across the bottom of the pull-down stairs to keep them from scraping the hallway carpet. When Katherine called him for dinner, he left his power drill and other tools in the attic and climbed down the stairs. After dinner, he went into the den and watched television. Meanwhile, Katherine went to the upstairs bedroom and began reading a book. A few minutes later, she heard someone turn the drill off and on. She walked into the hallway and found the drill lying on its side, propped up against the wall. Katherine ran downstairs and told her husband about her strange experience, but he could find nothing out of the ordinary.

Katherine had another paranormal experience a few weeks later. "I had just gotten over the drill business," she said, "when I went upstairs to watch television one night. I was completely engrossed in a TV drama when I began to hear what sounded like static electricity in the middle of the room—a kind of popping in the air." She turned off the television, but as she walked around the room, the same noise seemed to be following her. As she backed up into a corner of the room, the noise seemed to move up into her face. Frantically, she ducked under the noise and ran down the stairs. The noise remained upstairs.

James had his own encounter in the house in 1988. At the time, he was in the habit of waking up early in the morning and walking downstairs to the family room, where he read the morning newspaper. If Katherine needed him, she rang a little "angel bell" by her bedside. "One morning, he heard the bell ringing and came upstairs. But I was still asleep," Katherine said. "He couldn't figure it out."

House guests of the Tatums heard a different kind of ringing noise. The Tatums were staying at the couple's house in Florida while their guests stayed in the Tatums' house. Sometime during the night, the visitors were awakened by a loud ringing sound, like an alarm clock. They looked all over the house but could not find the source of the noise. They reported the incident to James and Katherine the next morning. The best explanation they could give their house guests was that the disturbances were probably connected to the Civil War history of the property. Their visitors did not find this news to be very comforting.

The Lost Confederate Treasury

Wilkes County

On April 2, 1865, Confederate president Jefferson Davis was on his way home from church when he received word that General Robert E. Lee's defensive line had been breached and Union forces were converging on Richmond. Davis informed the members of his cabinet that they should leave Richmond immediately and take the Confederate treasury and the assets of six banks with them on two trains on the line connecting Richmond and Danville, Virginia. The Confederate treasury, which amounted to $500,000, consisted of gold double eagle coins, gold ingots, silver coins and bricks and $200,000 worth of Mexican silver dollars. The treasury was packed away into wooden crates and loaded on the train. The first train, which the cabinet members had boarded, left that evening. The second train, which carried the hard currency, was commanded by navy captain William H. Parker. Because most of the Confederate army was still trying to hold off the Yankees, the men guarding the shipment of gold and silver were young, inexperienced sailors from a training ship in the Hames River.

When the first train came to a dead stop in Danville, Davis and his cabinet continued their journey on horse. Captain Parker ordered the midshipmen to load the treasury onto wagons, which would carry it to the old U.S. Mint at Charlotte, North Carolina. To avoid capture by the Union army, Captain Parker zigzagged the wagons across the South Carolina–Georgia state line. Captain Parker and Jefferson Davis met up again in a camp outside Washington, Georgia. They decided to deposit the money in a bank at Washington. An undetermined amount of money was handed out as payment to the soldiers. A few days later, when the money was counted, approximately $200,000 was missing. While it is true that some money had been exchanged for Confederate bills in Danville, the amount did not come even close to $200,000. Rumors soon spread that the money had been removed from the train and concealed somewhere in Danville.

On May 24, 1865, the wagons arrived at the Chennault plantation in Washington. At 11:00 p.m., members of the Seventh and Eighth Tennessee, which had switched sides from the Union to the Confederacy, attacked the wagon train, stuffing gold coins in their saddlebags. One of the saddlebags had a hole in it and leaked a trail of gold coins. The soldiers, under the command of Union general Edward A. Wild, tortured the male members of the Chennault family and strip-searched the women. General Wild searched the Chennault plantation for Confederate treasure but found nothing. When General Ulysses Simpson Grant learned of General Wild's mistreatment of the Chennault family, he relieved Wild of his command. Approximately $250,000 was lost in the attack, some of which is believed to have been buried somewhere in Wilkes County.

Some of the money stolen by the bushwhackers—approximately $11,000—was recovered by bank officials. When Jefferson Davis was apprehended on May 10, 1865, he had only a handful of dollars in his possession. The fate of the Confederate treasury is still unknown. However, for many years, local residents have been passing down stories of gold coins washing out of the hillside following heavy rains.

Another story focuses on the Mumfords, a family of Confederate sympathizers who also lived in Wilkes County. According to the website historynaked.com, a portion of the Confederate treasury was handed out to Davis's cabinet members during their final meeting. One of these men was a Confederate sympathizer from New York named Sylvester Mumford. Supposedly, he took part of his share of the treasury to Great Britain. Following Mumford's death, the remainder of his share of the treasury was passed down to his daughter, Goertner "Gertrude" Mumford Parkhurst, who lived in New York. She established a foundation for the descendants of Confederate soldiers. This story became popular in Georgia following the publication of Martha Mizell Puckett's book *Snow White Sands* in 1975.

The Roswell Mill Ruins

ROSWELL

The Roswell Manufacturing Company Mills were constructed on Vickery Creek between 1839 and 1853. The creek was dammed to create a waterfall that produced water power for the mill. The Roswell Mills produced wood and cotton, which was used to make Confederate uniforms. General Sherman ordered the Union army to burn the mill on July 7, 1864. The four hundred millworkers, most of whom were women and children, were deported to the North on trains. The cotton mills and woolen factory were rebuilt in 1882 but severely damaged by fire once again in 1926, this time by lightning. Southern Mills bought the old mill in 1947. Roswell Mills

Some of the machinery that was destroyed by the Union army is scattered along the banks of the creek.

The unquiet spirits of the women and children who work at the mill can still be heard in the machine shop.

continued operations until 1975, when competition from overseas forced it to close. Today, the Roswell Mills are controlled by the U.S. National Park Service.

Most of the paranormal activity reported at the Roswell Mills ruins revolves around the unquiet spirits of the millworkers. Dianna Avena, author of *Roswell: History, Haunts and Legends*, says that many people have heard the clanging sounds of machinery. Visitors have reported seeing the apparitions of women and children walking around the banks of the creek and hearing bloodcurdling screams coming from the machine shop, the only one of the original mill buildings still standing. Are these the cries of millworkers who were injured while operating the machinery?

LEGENDARY BAD MEN (AND WOMEN)

THE ATLANTA RIPPER

ATLANTA

Years before the term "serial killer" was coined, newspapers in England and America capitalized on the grisly murders of women by solitary killers who were probably psychopathic. The most infamous of these butchers, Jack the Ripper, murdered at least five women in London's Whitechapel district between 1888 and 1891. These unsolved murders have tantalized crime buffs for over a century. Unknown to many people today is an equally horrifying killing spree that terrorized the inhabitants of Atlanta between 1911 and 1912.

According to an article posted in American Hauntings, the Atlanta Ripper, as this psychopath was christened in the newspapers, claimed his first victim in May 1911. An article published in the *Atlanta Constitution* on May 29, 1911 reported that the body of an African American woman named Belle Walker was discovered by her sister not far from Belle's home. Belle's throat had been cut on her way home from the residence where she worked as a cook. Two weeks later, following the murder of another Black woman, Addie Watts, a four-paragraph article in the *Atlanta Journal* speculated that Walker and Watts had been murdered by the same person. The writer also noted the similarity between the Jack the Ripper murders and the Atlanta murders. On July 1, 1911, a twenty-year-old African American woman named Emma Lou Sharpe had an encounter with the Atlanta Ripper and miraculously survived. She was on her way home from the market to look for her mother, Lena, who had gone there to buy groceries an hour or so before. Suddenly, a tall Black man with broad shoulders approached her. He asked her how she was feeling. She said that she was fine and attempted to walk away, but he stabbed her in the back. Screaming, Emma ran off and found help. However, her relief immediately turned to sorrow after learning that someone, probably the same man who had attacked her, had cut her mother's throat to the bone.

Twenty-two-year-old Mary Yeldell almost became the Atlanta Ripper's third victim on July 8, 1911. On her way home from the residence of W.M. Selcer, where Mary worked as a cook, she had just passed an alley when she noticed a tall Black man moving toward her quickly. Mary turned and ran back to the Selcer residence on Fourth Street as fast as she could go. Mr. Selcer saw her coming and quickly ushered Mary into the house. He then ordered the man to raise his hands, but the strange Black man ran back down the alley. His streak of Saturday-night attacks had ended.

Alarmed by the growing number of attacks on African American women, local Black churches offered a reward for the apprehension of the Atlanta Ripper. However, the offer of the reward did not deter the Atlanta Ripper. On July 11, 1911, a crew of sewer workers followed a blood trail to a small ditch where they found the mutilated corpse of Sadie Holley, whose head was almost decapitated. Her shoes were nowhere to be found. The combs she wore were discovered on Atlanta Avenue. Because of the large number of Saturday-night murders, Holley was labeled the seventh victim by some newspapers and the eighth victim by others.

Not long after this latest murder, the police apprehended two suspects. A twenty-seven-year-old worker named Henry Huff who was seen with Holley the night she died was found wearing blood-smeared clothes. A short while later, another man who was seen with the victim that night, Todd Henderson, was arrested on Saloon Street. Because the evidence pointing to the men was largely circumstantial, the police were not totally convinced that they had found the murderers.

Their suspicions were proven to be well founded when, six weeks later, the body of twenty-year-old Mary Ann Duncan was found along the railroad tracks in an area known as Blanctown. Then, on November 10, Minnie Wise's body was discovered in an alley. In both cases, the young women's throats had been slashed.

Despite May Winn's assertion in a letter to a detective agency that Atlanta was one of the safest major cities in the country, terror spread through the Black community. African American churches collected a $12,000 reward for the apprehension of the Atlanta Ripper. Meanwhile, the murders continued unabated. In April 1912, a nineteen-year-old girl was found in some bushes on Pryor Street. The body of the twentieth victim, a fifteen-year-old "pretty octoroon," was pulled out of the Chattahoochee River not long thereafter.

After a number of Black men were arrested on suspicion of committing the Atlanta Ripper murders, Henry Brown was charged with the murder of Eva Florence from November. The arrest was based largely on the testimony of his wife, who said that her husband had come home several Saturdays with blood on his clothes. Brown confessed to the murder following intense questioning. However, during the trial, a man named John Rutherford testified that police had beaten a confession out of the man. The revelation, together with Brown's statement that he often suffered from hallucinations, led to his acquittal on October 18.

Unable to locate the real Atlanta Ripper, the police finally declared that the murder spree had ended after the death of the twenty-first victim, a nineteen-year-old light-skinned Black woman. Many residents were not surprised, however, when another Black woman was murdered within the next few months after the announcement by the police. The body of a "mulatto" girl named Laura Smith, who worked as a servant, turned up in March 1913. One year later, firefighters found several disturbing notes on fireboxes. The writer promised to "cut the throats of all negro women." Nothing more was heard from the Atlanta Ripper after the discovery of the notes, and the murders soon faded from the newspapers and the public memory. Today, many citizens of Atlanta wonder if these horrific murders would still be unsolved if the victims had been white.

Anjette Donovan Lyles, Georgia's Female Serial Killer

MACON

Anjette Lyles, Macon's most famous serial killer, was born Anjette Donovan in 1925. According to the website Headstuff.org, she was the spoiled daughter of affluent parents. She soon learned how to talk people into giving her what she wanted. In 1947, Anjette married Ben Lyles, a World War II veteran. One year later, she went to work in the Lyles family's restaurant after the birth of her daughter Marcia. Most of the time, Anjette worked alongside her mother-in-law, Julia, who took over the restaurant after the death of Ben's father. Anjette became the sole breadwinner of her family due to the debilitating effects of the rheumatic fever her husband contracted during the war. Ben's pain and alcoholism made it impossible for him to work. Fortunately, Anjette's business acumen, along with her personal charm, helped make the restaurant a success. In 1951, the debts Ben had incurred as a result of his gambling addiction drove him to sell the restaurant for only $2,500 while Anjette was giving birth to her second daughter, Carla. The hard times resulting from the loss of the family's business became even harder after the Veterans' Administration reduced her pension by 90 percent. A few months later, Ben was afflicted with nosebleeds and seizures. Eventually, he sank into a coma and died on January 25, 1952.

Now a single mother, Anjette went to work at another restaurant. By April 1955, she had earned enough to buy back the family restaurant for five times the price Ben had sold it for. For a while, the future seemed bright for Anjette. She hired her former mother-in-law to work in the restaurant. Anjette soon became involved with one of her customers, a pilot named Joe "Buddy" Neal Gabbet. After vacationing in Texas and New Mexico, the couple married. Although Anjette and her new husband were, to all appearances, very happy together, rumors spread that she was seeing other men during his frequent absences. Some people even believed that Anjette was dabbling in the occult, largely because she took some of her friends to see fortunetellers. Her marital bliss began to unravel when Buddy developed a strange rash that covered his entire body. He died on December 3, 1955. His doctors were puzzled by Anjette's refusal to grant an autopsy. With the money from Buddy's insurance policy, Anjette bought a new house and car.

Ben's mother agreed to help with her granddaughters. Anjette's insistence that her former mother-in-law make out a will led to squabbles between the two women. Then in the summer of 1957, Julia suddenly started vomiting blood and was admitted to the hospital. She died on September 29, 1957, leaving one-third of her $11,000 estate to her other son, Joseph; one-third to Anjette; and one-third to be split between Marcia and Carla.

Over the next few months, Anjette's relationship with Marcia deteriorated. In March 1958, Marcia was sitting in the restaurant when she started coughing uncontrollably. Anjette's home remedy of whiskey and a spoonful of sugar only aggravated Marcia's symptoms. Following a bout of vomiting, Marcia was admitted to the hospital. The fruit drinks Anjette brought the nine-year-old did not seem to help. Marcia began complaining of hallucinations. Her doctors diagnosed her with kidney failure, although they really had no idea what was wrong with the child. She died on April 5, 1958. The autopsy revealed no evidence of kidney failure.

The coroner's curiosity as to the cause of the mysterious deaths of Anjette's loved ones was piqued by the arrival of a letter by one of Anjette's employees at the restaurant. According to the anonymous writer of the letter, Anjette claimed that she had bought ant poison because of an infestation at the restaurant, even though no ants were ever reported by the employees or customers. The coroner analyzed the brand of ant poison that Anjette had in her house and discovered that it contained arsenic. He then informed Anjette and Carla that Marcia might have accidentally ingested ant poison. Carla confessed, rather unconvincingly, that she had given the poison to her sister while playing doctor. Convinced that Anjette was probably behind the four strange deaths in her family, the authorities arrested her in the hospital while she was being treated for an inflamed varicose vein. She was arraigned on four counts of murder but was indicted only for the murder of her daughter.

Anjette's trial in October 1958 soon became a media sensation throughout Georgia. Anjette testified that Julia had confessed to the murders in a letter found by her maid. However, her maid testified that Anjette had attempted to force her to testify that she had found the letter in Julia's purse. Handwriting experts proved not only that the letter was a forgery but also that the signature on Julia's will was a forgery by the same person. This evidence, together with the weak defense by Anjette's lawyer—that alcohol poisoning was the cause of Ben's death and that Buddy contracted the rash before marrying Anjette—convinced the jury that she was guilty. Anjette was sentenced to death and placed on death row by Governor Ernest Vandiver. However, she was granted a stay of execution after being diagnosed as schizophrenic and was committed to the Milledgeville state hospital, where she was confined for eighteen years. In 1977, Anjette died of a heart attack at age fifty-two.

JOHN HENRY "DOC" HOLLIDAY

VALDOSTA

John Henry Holliday, better known as "Doc" Holliday, has become one of the most iconic figures in the history and lore of the Old West. Stricken with tuberculosis, Holliday moved west in the hope that the arid climate would help relieve his symptoms. He and a friend named John A. Seegar set up a dental practice in Dallas, Texas, in September 1873. However, Holliday had to leave Dallas because of a gunfight with a saloon owner. Over the next few years, he was forced to move from town to town because of his penchant for gambling and his growing reputation as a gunslinger, probably because his constant coughing made it difficult for him to practice dentistry anywhere but in saloons. For a time, he settled in Dodge City, Kansas, where he opened another dental practice out of his rooms. At this time, he and his lover, Kate Elder, began passing themselves off as husband and wife. In 1878, Holliday intervened in a shootout between Wyatt Earp and several cowboys in Dodge City. Convinced that Holliday had saved his life, Earp became Holliday's closest friend. Eventually, Earp and Holliday ended up in Tombstone, Arizona. On October 26, 1881, Holliday fought alongside Wyatt and his two brothers, Virgil and Morgan, in the most famous gunfight in the Old West: the gunfight at the O.K. Corral. In less than a minute, three were dead and two were wounded. Afterward, Holliday moved to Colorado. On November 8, 1887, Holliday finally succumbed to tuberculosis in Glenwood Springs, Colorado, at the age of thirty-six.

This is the Doc Holliday that has become part of the romanticized West. The part of his life that is not nearly as well known is his early years in Georgia, much of which is shrouded in mystery. John Henry Holliday was born in Griffin, Georgia, on August 14, 1851, to Henry Burroughs Holliday and Jane McKey Holliday. In 1864, they moved to Valdosta, where the boy became one of the first students at Valdosta Institute. By the time he graduated, he had a classical education in history, mathematics, Latin and French. At the age of eighteen, Holliday was enrolled in the Pennsylvania College of Dental Surgery. After graduating in 1872, he was apprenticed to Dr. Lucian Frederick Fink in Valdosta before setting up his own practice in Atlanta a few months later.

A number of questions related to Holliday's early life remain unanswered. Some historians believe that he contracted tuberculosis from his mother, who died of the disease in 1866 when he was fifteen years old. However,

Doc Holliday's spirit seems to have a ghostly connection to the Holliday-Dorsey-Fife House in Fayetteville. *Wikimedia Commons.*

because he did not develop a bad cough until he started practicing dentistry in Atlanta, it is possible that he could have contracted the disease from a different person. Another unverified story comes from family folklore. Some of Holliday's family members passed down the story that he was involved in a shooting on the Withlacoochee River, just northeast of Valdosta, when he was a teenager. They also say that he may have shot and killed one or more African Americans. One of the persistent legends circling around Holliday's Georgia years has to do with his connection to Margaret Mitchell, author of the novel *Gone with the Wind*. According to the website valdostamuseum.com, Holliday's first cousin Martha Ann "Mattie" Holliday served as the model for Mitchell's character Melanie Hamilton. A good friend of Doc Holliday's, Martha, her mother and her siblings stayed in Henry B. Holliday's house from 1864 until the end of the Civil War in 1865. Later, Martha joined the Order of the Sisters of Mercy and wrote to Holliday throughout his entire life. It is also interesting to note that Phillip Fitzgerald, the uncle-in-law of one of Doc's uncles, Robert Kennedy Holliday, was Margaret Mitchell's great-grandfather.

Doc Holliday's strong attachment to Mattie Holliday might explain the paranormal activity that has been reported at the Holliday-Dorsey-Fife House in Fayetteville. In her book *Georgia Ghosts*, author Nancy Roberts reports that the specter of a handsome young man wearing black boots and a broad-brimmed hat has been sighted leaning against the columns of the house or walking through the yard. Could this be the spirit of Doc Holliday, who is still drawn to Mattie's former home?

LEGENDARY CEMETERIES

BONAVENTURE CEMETERY

SAVANNAH

The land on which the cemetery was founded was originally part of a six-hundred-acre plantation owned by Colonel John Mulryne. On March 10, 1846, Peter Wiltberger purchased the plantation and its family cemetery from Commodore Josiah Tattnall. The burials of people outside the Mulryne family began four years later. After Peter Wiltberger was entombed in the cemetery, his son Major William H. Wiltberger established the Evergreen Cemetery Company on June 12, 1868. When the City of Savannah acquired the cemetery on July 7, 1907, the name was changed to Bonaventure Cemetery. A number of local and national celebrities are buried here, including poet and novelist Conrad Aiken (1889–1973), singer/songwriter Johnny Mercer (1904–1976) and philanthropist Mary Telfair (1791–1875). Today, the cemetery is known not only for its beauty but for its ghost legends as well.

The cemetery's oldest ghost story dates back to the time when Colonel John Mulryne owned the property. The story goes that on the night of the Harvest Moon, sometime in the late eighteenth century, the Mulrynes hosted a grand masquerade party. According to legend, the party was in full swing when a servant rushed over to Colonel Mulryne and reported that the

Johnny Mercer's tombstone is etched with the titles of some of his best-known songs, such as "Moon River," "Autumn Leaves" and "On the Atchison, Topeka, and Santa Fe."

Bonaventure Cemetery is located on the site of a plantation once owned by John Mulryne.

Visitors to the cemetery have heard the spectral sounds of ghostly laughter and crackling flames.

kitchen had caught fire and the flames were beginning to spread. Instead of panicking, Mulryne ordered the servants to carry the chairs, tables, food and wine outside the home. As the fire engulfed the plantation house, the owners and their guests feasted and drank, basking in the glow of the flames. At the end of the feast, the master and his guests threw their glasses against a tree. Today, some of the visitors to the cemetery claim that they have heard the sounds of crackling of flames, tinkling of glass and spectral laughter.

One of the best-known—and most poignant—of Bonaventure's ghost stories begins with the birth of Gracie Watson in Massachusetts on July 10, 1885. Her parents, Wales J. and Frances Watson, operated the Pulaski Hotel at the corner of Bull and Bryan Streets. Under their management, the Pulaski became one of the best hotels in the entire South. Gracie endeared herself to everyone she met. Guests enjoyed watching the little girl sing and dance in the lobby. Before long, Gracie became the unofficial greeter in the Pulaski Hotel. When she took ill and died from pneumonia two days before Easter in 1889, the entire city mourned. Understandably, her parents were heartbroken, especially her father, who sank into a deep depression. Gracie was interred in the Bonaventure Cemetery. A sculptor named John Walz created a statue of the little girl using a photograph as a model. Her ghost has been seen walking around the graveyard, skipping and dancing, like any normal little girl.

Not long after Gracie's funeral, her father quit his job as manager of the Pulaski Hotel. After managing the Desoto Hotel for a short while, he and his wife returned to New England, leaving their little daughter all alone in Savannah.

Sightings of the little girl's ghost would indicate that she is still happy in her adopted home. Many people have also seen her playing in Johnson Square, where the Pulaski Hotel once stood. At first, eyewitnesses believed that she was a flesh-and-blood child running through the square in a white dress until she suddenly disappeared.

COLONIAL PARK CEMETERY

SAVANNAH

Founded in 1750 at Abercorn and Oglethorpe Streets, Colonial Park Cemetery is the oldest, as well as one of the most haunted, graveyards in Savannah. Other burial grounds existed before Colonial Park Cemetery, but many of them were paved over as the city expanded. Because some people were buried in mass graves and many grave markers have been destroyed over time, only one thousand of the ten thousand people interred in the cemetery are in marked graves. In 1864, a large number of General Sherman's troops camped out in the cemetery. To pass the time, they changed the dates on some of the gravestones. This sacred place was also a popular dueling spot in the eighteenth and early nineteenth centuries. Governor David B. Mitchell outlawed dueling in 1809, but duels continued to be fought in the state until 1877. According to the Ghost City Tours article titled "The Ghosts of Colonial Park Cemetery," the desecration of the graveyard accounts for the large amount of paranormal activity there.

One of the cemetery's best-known ghosts is the spirit of a seven-foot-tall giant named Rene Rondelier. Born in 1777, Rene became infamous for his psychotic behavior at a young age. He was said to have mutilated and killed dozens of animals in the cemetery. Attempts were made to curtail his nightly forays into the cemetery and elsewhere by erecting a wall around his

The desecration of consecrated ground during the Civil War may have turned Colonial Park Cemetery into one of Savannah's most haunted burial grounds.

Mists and apparitions have been sighted floating around the tombstones for many years.

house. However, the builders failed to take into account his brute strength. Before long, he broke out of his enclosure and escaped. When the bodies of two girls were discovered outside the cemetery gates with their throats cut, locals were convinced by the trail of oversized footprints that Rondelier was responsible. A lynch mob apprehended him with a great deal of effort and transported him to a swamp, where he was hanged. Legend has it that for many years, his large, shadowy form has been sighted prowling around Colonial Park Cemetery, even though no historical evidence has ever been found that substantiates the existence of Rene Rondelier.

Guests taking tours through Colonial Park Cemetery claim to have had ghostly experiences there. Spectral shapes have been sighted flitting around the tombstones. Eerie noises have sent shivers down the spines of late-night visitors. Some people even claim to have seen a green mist hovering around the tombstones.

MARIETTA NATIONAL CEMETERY

MARIETTA

The fact that ten thousand Union soldiers are buried in Marietta National Cemetery is ironic, considering that the Union army under the command of General Sherman laid siege to the town for five months before General Hugh Kirkpatrick set fire to it in November 1864. In 1866, a local merchant and Union sympathizer named Henry Cole offered a large plot of land for use as a burial ground for Union soldiers who had died in Sherman's Atlanta Campaign. Following the purchase of additional acreage in 1870, the cemetery reached its present size of twenty-three acres. The cemetery's archway is one of five monumental archways found in the South.

In her book *Haunted Marietta*, author Rhetta Akamatsu writes that Marietta National Cemetery is a very active paranormal site. Most of the haunted activity that has been reported seems to be residual in nature. Apparitions of sentries have been seen patrolling the area. People have heard the reports of pistols and rifles. The beating of drums and the sounds of marching feet resound through the cemetery on occasion.

Many of the Union soldiers who died in Sherman's Atlanta Campaign are buried in Marietta National Cemetery.

MEMORY HILL CEMETERY

MILLEDGEVILLE

When the Milledgeville town plan was created in 1803, the plot of land where Memory Hill Cemetery is now located was originally designated as a town square. After the cemetery opened in 1804, the area was called Cemetery Square. Because Milledgeville was the state capital from 1807 to 1868, several legislators are buried here, including Congressman Carl Vinson. Other luminaries include western outlaw Bill Miner, seer Dixie Haygood and author Flannery O'Connor.

The cemetery's most legendary grave is the tomb of Sarah Fish. The story goes that after she died, her husband, William Fish, was so despondent that he decided he did not want to live without her. One night, he entered his wife's tomb and placed a rocking chair next to her casket. Then he sat in the chair and rocked until he died. Today, some people say that if you walk up to Sarah Fish's tomb and ask in a loud voice, "Mr. Fish, what are you doing in there?" he replies, "Nothing."

OAKLAND CEMETERY

ATLANTA

Atlanta Cemetery was founded in 1850 on six acres. It was renamed in 1872 because of all the oak trees growing on the plot. The gates and surrounding walls were added in 1896. One section contains the graves of soldiers who died in the area's military hospitals. The graves of approximately four thousand soldiers who died in Sherman's invasion of Atlanta are here as well. Around three thousand of the soldiers in this section are unknown. German Jewish members of the Benevolent Congregation were buried in the "New" Jewish section between 1878 and 1892. Approximately seventeen thousand people are interred in the Potter's Field. Many of the graves in the Black section are unmarked because their wooden markers rotted away years ago. The Bell Tower, which now houses the offices of the historic Oakland Foundation, originally served as the sexton's office.

The tornado that ravaged Atlanta on March 14, 2008, toppled and damaged monuments through the cemetery. Perhaps this is the reason why so many of the spirits in Oakland Cemetery seem to be restless. Many of the

Some of the ghosts of the soldiers buried at Oakland Cemetery are unable to enjoy their eternal rest. *Wikimedia Commons.*

ghosts in the cemetery are the spirits of soldiers. One of the many visitors in the cemetery reported hearing a spectral roll call in the Confederate section. Others have heard disembodied voices calling out for friends and relatives.

OCONEE HILL CEMETERY

ATHENS

At the urging of the University of Georgia's trustees, the City of Athens purchased seventeen acres of land near the Oconee River. In 1856, a board of trustees was created to oversee the cemetery. By 1896, all of the lots were sold, at least in part because of the cemetery's scenic beauty. To meet the growing demand for lots, the city increased the size of the cemetery by eighty-two acres. A bridge connecting the old section with the new section was erected in 1899. Unlike many cemeteries of that period, Oconee Hill Cemetery accepted all races. A large number of burials from the Old Athens Cemetery were exhumed and moved to Oconee Hill Cemetery.

A ghostly carriage appears on the bridge in Oconee Cemetery.

Oconee Hill Cemetery's most famous haunting is a spectral carriage that has been sighted on the bridge. According to legend, a drunken farmer was driving his carriage through the cemetery when his wagon veered off the bridge. He died in the accident. His ghost is seen when the moon is full, attempting to complete his unfinished business, whatever it was.

ST. JAMES EPISCOPAL CEMETERY

MARIETTA

Located at the corner of Winn and Polk Streets, St. James Episcopal Cemetery was founded in 1849 on a corner of the grounds of St. James Episcopal Church. A number of famous people have been interred here over the years, such as John Glover, the first mayor of Marietta, and Rip Blair, who transformed Marietta into an industrial center. The most famous

Marion Meinert's tombstone in St. James Episcopal Cemetery has been the stuff of legend for generations.

burial in the cemetery is that of six-year-old JonBenét Ramsey, who was bludgeoned to death in her hometown of Boulder, Colorado, on December 26, 1996. She is buried next to her mother, Patsy Ramsey, and her half sister, Elizabeth Ramsey.

Down through time, fascinating stories have attached themselves to some of the lesser-known graves in the cemetery. The southwestern corner is believed to contain the unmarked graves of slaves, although no historical proof has surfaced. The most legendary grave is that of Marion Meinert, whose monument stands near the grave of JonBenét Ramsey. A member of the Marietta Society, she died of tuberculosis in 1898. Her husband lies next to her under a large cross. The statue on Marion's monument depicts her holding two infants, leading some locals to speculate that her grave is haunted because she died in childbirth. Others say she was consumed by flames while trying to rescue her children from their burning home. Young people who venture out to the cemetery late at night claim to have heard crying sounds coming from the monument. Some say that they have seen blood trickling from the eyes of her statue onto her bodice. According to another legend, one can summon Marion's ghost on Halloween night by standing before her statue and asking, "Mary, Mary, how did your children die?"

LEGENDARY LOCATIONS

THE ANDREW LOW HOUSE

SAVANNAH

Andrew Low emigrated from Scotland at the age of sixteen with the hope of making a fortune in America. He started out in his uncle's cotton business in Savannah, eventually working his way up to becoming a partner in the firm. Low's diligence and ambition led him to become one of the most successful cotton factors in the entire city. After marrying Sarah Cecil Hunter in 1843, he began planning a home worthy of a man of his status. In 1848, Low hired New York architect John Norris to design a mansion in the Italianate style for his wife and three children. Just before Low and his family could move into the house, his wife and young son contracted a disease and died. Five years later, Low took a second wife, Mary Cowper Stiles, whose father was William Henry Stiles, U.S. minister to Austria.

During the Civil War, Low's sympathies lay with the Confederacy. In 1862, he was accused of being an agent of the Confederacy operating in England. Low refused to deny the charge to protect the brother-in-law of his business partner, John Low, who was the real agent. According to the family legend, his wife concealed the incriminating documents in her coiled hairdo while her husband was sitting in a Boston jail. He eventually managed to escape and return to Savannah.

The Andrew Low House is haunted by a variety of ghosts.

Andrew and Mary Low's beautiful home became the showplace of Savannah. Invitations to their parties were highly coveted, due in large part to the Lows' hospitality. A number of celebrities attended their parties as well. One of Low's best friends, British novelist William Makepeace Thackery, visited the Andrew Low House between 1853 and 1856. In 1870, shortly before his death, Robert E. Lee and his daughter, Agnes, spent the night at the Andrew Low House during a visit to Savannah.

Andrew Low's fame was eclipsed by that of his daughter-in-law Juliette Gordon Low, who married Andrew's son William in 1886. The couple spent much of their marriage at their home in Warwickshire, England. Unfortunately, their marriage was not a happy one, due to her husband's infidelity. She finally agreed to her husband's request for a divorce in 1901 when she returned from a trip and found his mistress living in her home. However, he died of a stroke shortly before their divorce was finalized. She went on to create the organization for which she is remembered today: the Girl Scouts.

Remnants of the past can be found in more than just the antique furnishings of the Andrew Low House, which is known as one of Savannah's most haunted places. One of the most active spirits in the house is the ghost of "Old Tom," a butler who served the Low family all his life. In his book *Haunted Savannah*, author James Caskey says that the phantom footsteps that echo through the halls of the old mansion are believed to be the butler's way of showing that he is still on the job. A stickler for order, Old Tom is believed to be the spirit responsible for making certain that all of the household items are in their proper places. On rare occasions, his full-bodied apparition has been sighted staring down at guests from the top of the staircase.

Another male ghost that some say haunts the Andrew Low House is the spirit of a distinguished-looking older gentleman in an old-fashioned suit. Some eyewitnesses have assumed that this is the ghost of Robert E. Lee. However, one wonders why Lee's spirit would have forged such a close connection to a house that he visited only once.

One of the ghosts believed to have made the Andrew Low House their permanent residence is female. Some of the docents believe that the female apparition with blond hair that has been sighted on the first floor is the spirit of Mary Cowper Stiles. She is a melancholy spirit who is still mourning the loss of her children. The master bedroom on the second

The master bedroom is haunted by the spirits of Mary Cowper Stiles and Juliette Gordon Low.

"The Creepy Doll Room" is a favorite of visitors at the Andrew Low House.

floor where both Mary Cowper Stiles and Juliette Gordon Low passed away is quite possibly the most haunted room in the entire house. Guests and docents walking by the room have been overcome with an oppressive feeling of sadness. The unmistakable sounds of weeping have been heard inside the room as well.

Several of the rooms in the house are said to be haunted by unidentified spirits. Neighbors have heard the lilting tones of a piano coming from the parlor on the first floor when the house is empty. Interestingly enough, the antique piano in the parlor has not been in working order for many years. People passing by the gentleman's parlor on the first floor have detected the strong aroma of cigar smoke. Rose-scented perfume wafts through the rooms on the second floor as well. On the second floor, the "Creepy Doll Room" is filled with antique dolls and toys. The ghost of a little boy seems to be attracted to this room.

The Andrew Low House is one of the few historic homes in Savannah that is open in the evening to ghost tours. During these special tours, the docents emphasize the dark side of the historic home. It is small wonder that the old house has such a haunted reputation.

THE AUGUSTA COTTON EXCHANGE BUILDING

AUGUSTA

In the late 1870s, Augusta was the second-largest inland cotton market in the world. By 1885, eight cotton manufacturers were operating in Augusta. Enoch William Brown designed the Augusta Cotton Exchange Building in the mid-1880s. The ornamental iron elements in the building, such as the iron columns in the entrance, were cast by the foundry of Charles F. Lombard. The offices for the cotton brokers were located on the trading floor. Only men were allowed in the Cotton Exchange, probably because of cockfights and sports gatherings that were held there after hours. Because of the devastation caused by the boll weevil, Augusta's economic dependence on cotton began to decline. By 1964, the cotton exchange in Augusta had ceased operations. Bill Moore of Aiken, South Carolina, bought and restored the old cotton exchange building. The windows were repaired, and the paint was removed from the heart pine wood inside the

The Augusta Cotton Exchange Building is haunted by a mischievous ghost named Isabella.

building. For the next few years, the Augusta Metropolitan Convention and Visitors Bureau used the building as a welcome center. It is now a branch of Georgia Bank and Trust of Augusta.

Bank employees who work at the old cotton exchange have had to deal with an assortment of paranormal interruptions in their daily work routine. The ghost, whom the employees have named "Isabella," used the electric typewriter to make her presence known, even when it was unplugged and out of paper. People have heard the clicking of typewriter keys when no one else was around. Swivel chairs spun themselves around, and computers malfunctioned for no apparent reason. Tellers have learned that if they exclaim, in a loud voice, "Isabella, stop!" the activity ceases. One of the ladies believed that this was Isabella's way of "getting even" with the men who made the Augusta Cotton Exchange off-limits to women for many years.

Barnsley Gardens

Adairsville

Erecting buildings on sites revered by Native Americans is never a good idea, judging from the legends surrounding these structures. In 1844, Godfrey Barnsley built his house he called Woodlands on a location sacred to the Cherokees, despite the warnings of a local Indian. According to the website Hauntedjourneys.com, the old house was afflicted with a series of misfortunes during its long history. Barnsley's wife, Julia, was denied the privilege of living in her beautiful home because she died of tuberculosis before construction was completed in 1848. On May 17, 1864, a friend of Barnsley's attempted to warn him of the approaching Union troops, but he was killed before he could deliver the message. By the time the Battle of Adairsville ended, Barnsley's mansion had been severely damaged. Before moving to New Orleans to recoup his wealth, Barnsley buried his loyal friend behind the mansion and turned over control of the plantation to his son-in-law, James Peter Baltzelle. Even though Baltzelle was not a blood relative of Godfrey Barnsley, he, too, fell victim to the family curse when a tree fell on top of him and killed him in 1868. Over the next five years, Barnsley tried unsuccessfully to make money. When he died in 1873, he had little money to his name. Barnsley was buried in the family cemetery. The house was passed down to Baltzelle's only daughter, Addie,

The ruins of Woodlands Plantation at Barnsley Gardens are haunted by the ghosts of Godfrey and Julia Barnsley. *Wikimedia Commons.*

who married B.F. Saylor in 1897. In 1906, her family was forced to move into the kitchen when a tornado destroyed the roof of the mansion. One of her sons, Preston, became a heavyweight boxer in the 1920s, fighting under the name K.O. Duggan. Over time, he suffered irreparable brain damage in the ring and was committed to an insane asylum. His brother Harry, whom Preston blamed for committing him to the state hospital, was unable to realize his dream of restoring Woodlands. Preston escaped from the hospital on March 13, 1935, and shot Harry in a heated argument over property rights on November 5, 1935. Harry died in his mother's arms in the front room. Preston was sent to prison on November 17, 1936, and was paroled in January 1943. The house passed out of the family when it was sold at auction. The new owners, who used the property primarily for farming, allowed the house to fall into ruin. Today, Barnsley Gardens is a lavish resort, designed to resemble an English village. Visitors enjoy such amenities as a pool, spa and, of course, the ghost stories.

The ruins of Woodlands Plantation still stand as a stark reminder of the location's tragic history. The ghosts of Godfrey and Julia Barnsley have been frequently sighted in the ruins of their former home. In her article "The Folklore and Legends of Barnsley Gardens," newspaper columnist Pam Walker includes a story she found in the family papers housed at Emory University in which Godfrey saw the ghost of his wife, Julia, standing by a fountain. Godfrey also received a handwritten letter from his deceased father-in-law, William Scarborough, in which he wrote, "Julia is with me and doing fine." Employees of the resort report seeing Godfrey's ghost stepping out of his library. He has also been seen strolling through the gardens at night with the ghost of Julia. Phantom footsteps have been heard inside the ruins as well. One of the most startling ghost stories concerns Harry Saylor's encounter with his uncle George Barnsley. One day, Harry told his mother, Addie, that when the doorbell rang and he opened the door, his uncle George was standing on the stoop. Within a few seconds, he vanished. The next day, the family received a cablegram informing them that George Barnsley had died in South America at the same time that Harry opened the door the day before.

BULLOCH HALL

ROSWELL

Major James Stephens, a planter from the Georgia coast, was invited to settle in Roswell by Roswell King, the founder of the town. He constructed Bulloch Hall in the Greek Revival style in 1839. The house is considered by architects to be one of a handful of southern mansions that were built in the true temple form. Following the death of his first wife, Hester Amarintha "Hettie" Elliot, Stephens married his mother-in-law, Martha "Patsy" Stewart. The couple had four children: Anna, Martha "Mittie," Charles and Irvine. The thirty-one slaves who worked on the plantation raised cotton and various other crops. Major Stephens had an important connection to American history. On December 22, 1853, his daughter Mittie married Theodore Roosevelt Sr. Their son Theodore became the twenty-seventh president of the United States. In 1905, President Roosevelt visited Bulloch Hall and gave a speech in which he said he was proud to be "half Southern and half Northern." Mittie's other son, Elliott, was the father of Eleanor Roosevelt, the wife of President Franklin Delano Roosevelt. Bulloch Hall is noteworthy today for its reconstructed slave quarters and the fact that 142

Bulloch Hall has an important historical connection to former president Theodore Roosevelt.

The cries of the ghost of a fourteen-year-old slave girl have been heard coming from the well.

of the trees on the grounds are in the Historic Tree Register. Bulloch Hall is listed in the National Register of Historic Places.

The ghost that is said to haunt Bulloch Hall is the spirit of a fourteen-year-old slave girl who fell into the well in the 1850s. Her ghostly crying has been heard coming from the well, usually at night. Dianna Avena, author of *Roswell: History, Haunts and Legends*, suggests that the enslaved girl's spirit might be making her presence known inside the plantation house as well. Because her job was to make candles, which were used to light houses in the mid-nineteenth century, some people believe that she might be responsible for turning the lights back on inside Bulloch Hall after the docents have turned them off for the night. A docent who had noticed that the lights she had turned off in the house were back on returned to the house the next morning with several other people. They noticed immediately that the security system had not been activated during the night. Whoever—or whatever—turned the lights on the night before could not have been human.

CALLAWAY PLANTATION

WASHINGTON

Callaway Plantation consists of the main houses that were donated by the Callaway family in 1977. Later, several other historic buildings were relocated to the 56-acre site. In the eighteenth century, members of Fuller Earle Callaway and Cason Jewell Callaway's family immigrated to West Georgia. Thomas Edward Callaway started his plantation on 200 acres of land nine miles west of Washington, Georgia, in 1785. One of his descendants, Jobe Callaway, returned to the plantation after spending time in Chambers County, Alabama. Following Jobe's death at the plantation, his son Jacob grew cotton that he sold to England prior to the Civil War. His son Parker increased the size of the plantation to 3,060 acres. Following Parker's death, his son Aristides sold most of the additional property and used the proceeds to build the brick manor house in 1869. The Greek Revival mansion was listed in the National Register of Historic Places on April 11, 1972. In 1977, the Callaway family's connection to the plantation came to an end when Aristides's granddaughter Katie Mae Arnold Hardin donated her part to the City of Washington.

Four mounted Confederate soldiers were seen riding behind the Callaway Plantation. *Marilyn Brown.*

Rumors of hauntings at the Callaway Plantation grew after it was acquired by the city. The most haunted building is the brick manor house where the Callaways lived between 1869 and 1910. Because the house has no electricity or indoor plumbing and is furnished with antiques from the period when the Callaways lived there, the old house seems to be the ideal place where spirits from the past would feel comfortable. Indeed, on his website, Jimmie D. Davis says that the mansion is "allegedly the site of many Confederate ghostly spirit guests." In her book *Georgia Ghosts*, author Nancy Roberts wrote about an experience the caretaker had at Callaway Plantation in the 1990s. He said that he and Michael, a friend of his, spent the night at Michael's trailer after returning from a double date. Soon after falling asleep, they heard the frantic barking of dogs. The men dressed hastily and stepped outside. They walked in back of the trailer, where they saw four mounted soldiers wearing Confederate uniforms. The soldiers stopped riding briefly and stared at the two men. Then they turned their horses toward Washington and rode off.

One of the paranormal groups that have visited the house, the Georgia Paranormal Society, reported that the ghost of Martha Callaway has been seen in the floor-length mirror at the top of the staircase. Workers walking outside the building claim to have seen the apparition of a woman, possibly Martha Callaway, staring out of the upper left window. The presence of two antique coffins enhances the creepy vibe that many visitors have felt inside the historic house.

THE CENTRAL STATE HOSPITAL

MILLEDGEVILLE

To serve the growing numbers of individuals suffering from mental illness, the State of Georgia constructed the Milledgeville Lunatic Asylum on a two-thousand-acre site outside the city. It operated for a century. The hospital housed up to thirteen thousand patients during its peak in nearly two hundred buildings, making it one of the largest state hospitals in the entire country. A large number of the patients lived and died in the hospital. Approximately twenty-five thousand of them were interred on the grounds, many of them in unmarked graves. Over time, Central State Hospital acquired a fearsome

The spirits of former patients at Central State Hospital express themselves in a variety of strange sounds.

reputation. Doctors were said to have treated their patients through the use of shock therapy, ice baths, isolation therapy, electroconvulsive therapy and lobotomies. An article published in the *Atlanta Constitution* revealed that a staff of only forty-eight doctors looked after thousands of patients. At the time, none of the physicians were licensed psychiatrists. In the 1970s, Governor Jimmy Carter initiated the transfer of patients to state-of-the-art facilities. With the exception of a few administration buildings, Central State Hospital closed in 2010. The remaining buildings were abandoned. Many of them were boarded up.

According to author Mary Hallberg, locals have been circulating tales of ghostly activity inside the old state hospital for many years. They speak of hearing piercing screams and spectral voices coming from empty buildings. Visitors bold enough to walk down the deserted hallways claim to have been touched by invisible fingers and to have passed through cold spots on hot summer days. Some people swear that someone—or something—breathed on the back of their necks. The smell of rotting meat often fills the air. A couple of women were walking outside one of the abandoned buildings when objects were hurled at them from one of the upper floors. Stories such as these lead one to conclude that Central State Hospital might be abandoned by the living but not by the dead.

CRYSTAL LAKE

IRWIN COUNTY

For most Americans, the term "Crystal Lake" conjures up cinematic images of a masked maniac preying on helpless camp counselors. In Georgia, Crystal Lake was a privately owned water resort in Irwin County from the 1920s until 1998. In the nineteenth century, the lake bore the name of gristmill owner Willis Bone. The lake was seventy-five feet deep at its deepest point. Underground springs from the Alapaha River fed into the recreation area. A.N. Adcock was the first owner to exploit the lake's potential as a tourist destination. The name of the lake was changed to Crystal Lake after it became one of the most popular resorts in the area in the 1920s. Thousands of tourists traveled to Irwin County each summer to swim, fish, bowl, dance and water ski at the lake resort. Crystal Lake's biggest attrition was a giant water slide called the Slippery Dip.

By the 1990s, attendance at the resort had dwindled. It closed in 1998 after the parents of a child who drowned in the lake sued the resort. Over the years, a number of legends were generated to explain the alleged curse that plagued Crystal Lake. In an article that appeared in *Valdosta Today* in 2019, Charles Shiver relates the earliest of these tales. Willie Bone, a Cherokee Indian, was believed to have been a Union sympathizer who shared his tribe's hatred of slavery. One day, an elderly justice of the peace named Jack Walker was tracking a wild hog when he discovered a runaway slave named Toney hiding in Bone's gristmill. When Walker attempted to drag Toney out of the gristmill, Bone hit him in the head with a rock and buried him in the mud. A short while later, Walker regained consciousness and tried unsuccessfully to claw his way out of his muddy grave. The search party that was sent out to look for him discovered his hands sticking out of the mud. A jury convicted Bone of murder, and he was hanged by the side of the lake. After the trial, Toney was killed as well; his body was unceremoniously dumped in Bone Pond.

A supernatural epilogue to the tale can be found in some of the variants. Some people have seen the grasping hands of Toney's restless spirit reaching out from the lake. Bone's spirit has been sighted standing by a tree; Walker's spirit wanders on the sandy bank of the lake. The story goes that Bone Pond was enlarged after a sinkhole swallowed up the gristmill and filled the surrounding area with water. However, many locals believe that the gristmill was either relocated or disassembled and sold for scrap.

The Ezekiel Harris House

AUGUSTA

Ezekiel Harris was a tobacco merchant who came to Georgia from Edgefield, South Carolina, late in the eighteenth century. He envisioned Augusta growing up around a tobacco warehouse and inspection station and becoming a major city someday. Sometime around 1797, Harris built a three-story inn on top of a hill to provide a place for visiting tobacco planters to stay.

For years, the Ezekiel Harris House was misidentified as the McKay House, also known as the "White House." At the time of the Revolutionary War, the McKay House was a trading post. In 1780, Thomas Brown was appointed

Built in 1797, the Ezekiel Harris House is said to be haunted by ghosts of the thirteen Patriots who were hanged from the staircase.

supervisor of the Augusta region by Royal Governor James Wright. Because of his attempts to eradicate the Sons of Liberty, a contingent of Patriots living in Augusta tarred and feathered him. After his recovery in South Carolina, Brown took vengeance on several families in Augusta, confiscating their property and removing them from the area. On September 14, 1780, the commander of the Revolutionary forces in Augusta, Colonel Elijah Clarke, attacked Brown's stronghold at the McKay trading post. A few days later, Captain Ashby and twelve other Patriots were hanged from the staircase of the McKay trading post in retaliation for the losses suffered by the British during the siege. Legend has it that each of the prisoners represents one of the thirteen colonies that had risen up against Britain.

Because of the house's assumed Revolutionary War history, it was purchased and preserved by the Richmond County Historical Society in 1948. However, a study conducted by the State of Georgia in 1975 suggests that the McKay House might have stood somewhere in the vicinity of the Ezekiel Harris House, possibly across the street. It was probably destroyed during the Revolutionary War. In his article "Revisiting Ezekiel Harris—

The Ezekiel Harris House, Augusta, Georgia," author Lewis Powell IV states that following this study, the house was renamed the Ezekiel Harris House after the first owner. Interestingly enough, ghost stories about the McKay House dating back to the Revolutionary War are responsible for its haunted reputation.

According to Kathryn Tucker Windham, author of *13 Georgia Ghosts and Jeffrey*, the ghost stories connected to the Ezekiel Harris House stem from the hanging of the Patriots. For years, locals said that anyone who stood in the stairwell of the house and counted to thirteen could hear the ropes being stretched and the groans of the men as they swayed in the wind. A female ghost who has been sighted in the house was said to be the spirit of Mrs. Glass, whose two sons were among the group of Patriots who were executed on that fateful day back in 1780. However, Powell suggests that the ghost might be the spirit of Mrs. Ezekiel Harris, who died of breast cancer.

Prior to becoming a historical landmark, the Ezekiel Harris House was owned by two families. In the mid-nineteenth century, the Sibley Mill across the street bought the house and converted it into a boardinghouse. Thanks to the publicity afforded the house by writers like Kathryn Tucker Windham and a host of paranormal investigators, the Ezekiel Harris House is remembered today as one of the city's historically haunted houses.

THE GEORGIA GUIDESTONES

ELBERT COUNTY

In June 1979, a distinguished-looking, gray-haired man who identified himself as R.C. Christian showed up at the office of the Elberton Granite Finishing Company. He explained to Joe H. Fendley Sr., the president of the company, that he needed a large granite monument that would be inscribed with instructions that would guide the human race into an "age of reason." Over a period of several weeks, Fendley's company produced four large slabs of blue granite, as well as a capstone. During his meeting with the president of Granite City Bank, Wyatt Martin, Christian said that in the future, other conservative-minded individuals and groups would form a ring around the central guidestone. The 119-ton monolith was inscribed with four thousand sandblasted characters and letters, each of which was four inches in height. The engraved messages, written in Egyptian hieroglyphics,

Babylonian cuneiform, classical Greek and Sanskrit, can be placed in four categories: spirituality, man's relationship to nature, population control and world government. The ten guides include "Rule passion," "Unite humanity with a new language," "Avoid petty laws" and "Prize truth, beauty, and love." The five-acre cow pasture on which the structure was erected was believed by the Cherokee Indians to be the center of the world.

Needless to say, the "American Stonehenge," as the structure has come to be known, has stirred up considerable controversy. Some conspiracy experts have suggested that the stones were set up by the New World Order or Satanists. The true identity of the man who called himself R.C. Christian is still unknown.

THE HAMPTON LILLIBRIDGE HOUSE

SAVANNAH

In 1799, Hampton Lillibridge designed his Savannah home in a style reminiscent of an eighteenth-century seacoast house in Rhode Island. In the nineteenth century, the house served as the Lillibridge family's home and as a boardinghouse. The historic home continued to serve as a tenement house into the first half of the twentieth century. Around this time, a sailor was believed to have hanged himself in one of the guest rooms on the third floor. In 1963, Jim Williams, an antiques dealer featured in John Berendt's 1994 book *Midnight in the Garden of Good and Evil*, purchased the home and the house next to it.

Jim Williams is the source of most of the ghost stories people still tell about the Hampton Lillibridge House. Williams immediately set about moving the house three blocks away to 507 East St. Julian Street. As the house next door was being moved, one of the workers was killed. When the workers were preparing the foundation of the Hampton Lillibridge House for the move, they discovered an empty crypt. Williams traced the crypt back to the colonial period because of its tabby construction. The story goes that the workers sealed the crypt and covered it over with dirt.

Williams believed that tampering with the crypt was responsible for the paranormal activity inside the house after it was moved. Workers complained that when they returned to the site the next morning, their tools had been moved to a different spot from where they had left them the day before.

The haunted reputation of the Hampton Lillibridge House is based on the stories told by former owner Jim Williams.

People visiting and working in the house heard phantom footsteps and ghoulish laughter inside the house. Williams claimed to have seen a spectral, human-like figure move down a hallway and vanish through a closed door. One day while Jim was on a hunting trip, he received a phone call from one of his neighbors informing him that he and a friend heard the sounds of a party coming from Williams's supposedly empty house. The two men entered the house and heard someone walking around on the floor above them. They rushed up the stairs to investigate. Suddenly, one of the men was pulled across the floor by an invisible force to a large hole in the middle of the room. He probably would have been seriously injured if his friend had not pulled him to safety.

Williams called 911 several times while he lived in the house. On one occasion, a police officer responded to Williams's complaint that someone was walking around the house. When the officer arrived, they both heard footsteps upstairs. The officer rushed up the stairs and followed the sound to a closet door. He tried to open the door, but it was locked. When the officer turned to leave, the door opened on its own.

The paranormal activity in the Hampton Lillibridge House continued to interrupt Williams's sleep for several more weeks. One day, a dark figure appeared in a doorway and disappeared after a few seconds. On December 7, 1963, Williams asked an Episcopal bishop to exorcise his house. The ritual seemed to work for a while, but activity picked up considerably two weeks later. Williams became so desperate that by the time he decided to move out of the house, he was sleeping with a loaded pistol by his bedside.

The Hampton Lillibridge House might have been "the most haunted house in Savannah" at one time, but evidence has surfaced suggesting that this is not true anymore. According to the website ghostcitytours.com, the present owners have lived in the house for several decades without experiencing any kind of ghostly activity. Consequently, the stories people tell about no one being able to occupy the house for more than two years are apocryphal. The fact is that sometimes, hauntings simply stop for no apparent reason.

THE HAY HOUSE

MACON

William Butler Johnston, a Macon industrialist, built the home at 934 Georgia Avenue between 1855 and 1859 for his wife, Anne, and their six children. The Johnstons designed their nineteen-thousand-square-foot house in the Italian Renaissance Revival style to remind them of the time they spent in Italy. The house's most distinctive feature is its two-story octagonal cupola. The home's state-of-the-art technological amenities included central heat, a speaker-tube system connecting fifteen rooms, an in-house kitchen and an elaborate ventilation system. Following the death of Anne Johnston in 1896, the house was bequeathed to her daughter Mary Ellen and her husband, Judge William Felton. Parks Lee Hay and his wife, Maude, acquired the house after the deaths of Mr. and Mrs. Felton. They immediately began redecorating the mansion in an effort to bring it into the twentieth century. Following the deaths of Mr. Hay in 1957 and Mrs. Hay in 1962, their family set up the P.L. Hay Foundation and opened it as a house museum. The Hay House was designated a National Historic Landmark in 1974. Three years later, the house was transferred to the Georgia Trust for Historic Preservation.

The most haunted part of the Hay House is the third floor. *Wikimedia Commons.*

One would expect an old Victorian-era mansion like the Hay House to be haunted. According to staff and visitors, it certainly is, especially the third floor. People claim to have walked through cold spots and to have heard doors slamming and disembodied footsteps. The apparition of an elderly woman wearing a late nineteenth-century dress is said to wander around the house. Eerie moans come from the master bedroom occasionally. Some visitors have even felt someone breathing over their shoulder.

In 2010, Jimmy Cannon might have inadvertently captured the image of one of the ghosts while photographing a wedding. While posing a picture of the groom and his groomsmen in the master bedroom, Cannon, on a whim, placed an old top hat on the head of the groom. When Cannon downloaded the photographs on his computer after the wedding, he was surprised to find the blurry image of a man wearing a top hat by the door. "It lacks any real definitions of facial features," Cannon said. Katy Brown, the director of the Hay House, said that no one should have touched the hat, which belonged to Parks Lee Hay Sr. Cannon thinks that Hay's ghost manifested to protest the improper use of his hat in the photograph.

THE ISAIAH DAVENPORT HOUSE

SAVANNAH

Born in Little Compton, Rhode Island, in 1784, Isaiah Davenport learned the craft of carpentry while serving as an apprentice carpenter under his father. At the age of twenty-four, Davenport moved to Savannah to help rebuild houses that were destroyed in the Great Savannah Fire of 1796. Shortly after arriving in the city, he married Sarah Rosemund Clark. As time passed, the size of their family swelled to ten children. Due to the increasing demand for his services, Davenport hired several other carpenters and purchased ten slaves. In 1820, he built a beautiful mansion for himself and his family at 325 East State Street. However, Davenport's wealth was unable to ensure him and his family everlasting happiness. His death from yellow fever in 1827 forced his wife to convert his home into a boardinghouse. By the turn of the century, the Davenport House had been sectioned off into apartments. By the first half of the twentieth century, the house had declined to the point that by 1955, plans were underway to replace it with a parking lot. Just a few hours before the house was scheduled for destruction, it was saved by a women's club that renovated it over the next few years and turned it into a house museum in 1963. The women's club grew into the Historic Savannah Foundation, which went on to preserve a number of historic homes in the city.

The spirts that haunt the Isaiah Davenport House might have a connection to the various families who have lived there. The ghost of a small girl has been sighted both inside and outside the house. Her first reported appearance occurred one day when several tourists were being led through the house. Suddenly, one of the tourists asked the cashier in the gift shop if any reenactors were in the house. When she said no reenactors were present, the tourist replied that she saw a little girl wearing an old-fashioned dress playing with toys on the second floor. It turned out that several other people in the group saw the child as well. The casher did a walk-through of the house but found nothing out of the ordinary. In 2002, another tourist saw a little girl staring out of a second-floor window. She notified a tour guide, who caught a quick glimpse of the small specter out of the corner of her eye.

A feline apparition also seems to call the Isaiah Davenport House home. For years, a large yellow cat has been seen walking to the house, both back when it was an apartment house and now that it has become a museum. In her book *Savannah Specters*, Margaret Wayt DeBolt told the story of Robert

The Isaiah Davenport House is believed to be haunted by the ghosts of a little girl and a cat.

Chung Chan's encounter with the ghost cat. He had just opened the front door and stepped into the house when a large yellow cat zoomed past him and took off down the hallway. The cat shows up periodically in several rooms in the house as well. Interestingly enough, many of the eyewitnesses are children who have seen the cat in places where no one else sees the animal.

JEKYLL ISLAND CLUB RESORT

JEKYLL ISLAND

James Oglethorpe, the founder of the colony of Georgia, named the island after his friend Sir Joseph Jekyll. In 1792, Christophe DuBignon bought a large section of land on Jekyll Island. In 1879, one of his descendants, John Eugene DuBignon, converted Jekyll Island into an exclusive resort. Seven years later, the Jekyll Island Club took control of Jekyll Island. The people who flocked to the Jekyll Island Club represented some of the richest people in the world. In 1901, the Annex was constructed to provide accommodations for the club's guests. In 1910, another lavish addition, Cherokee, was built. It was the largest of the island's nineteen cabins. In 1926, the Great Dunes Golf Course was completed. Attendance at the club began dropping off during the Great Depression. During World War II, the federal government evacuated the island because of the threat from enemy submarines. After the government purchased the island in 1948 for $675,000, it became a state park. Restoration of the club began in 1985, and the Jekyll Island Club Resort opened in 1987.

Some of the former guests appear to have loved Jekyll Island so much that they never left. Wealthy banker J.P. Morgan may have become one of these resident spirits. As Morgan was accustomed to smoking an expensive cigar every morning at 5:00 a.m. in his room in the Annex when he was alive, his ghost is said to have kept up the habit. People have smelled the pungent odor of cigar smoke in his room at 5:00 a.m. Another rich guest, railroad magnate Samuel Spencer, may be haunting the hotel as well. In 1906, he died in a train accident. Guests staying in his former room claim to have found evidence that his ghost read their newspaper and drank their coffee, just as he did every morning when he was alive.

Named after a friend of James Oglethorpe, Sir Joseph Jekyll, in 1797, Jekyll Island became a resort in 1879. *Wikimedia Commons.*

Ghosts of wealthy guests and hotel staff are said to haunt the Jekyll Island Club. *Wikimedia Commons.*

One of the founding members of the club, General Lloyd Aspinwall, died on September 4, 1886, just one year before the club opened. Years later, the club received letters from members claiming to have seen the general's ghost at dusk, walking on the Riverfront Veranda near the sunroom that bears his name, the Aspinwall Room.

Ghosts of the rich and famous are not the only apparitions that disturb the tranquility of the hotel. A bellman wearing a uniform dating back to the 1920s has been sighted on the second floor of the club's main building. The fastidious spirit is known for his attention to detail. The night before weddings are held in the hotel, he has pressed the groom's suit and knocked on his door to make sure that he is awake. Not all of the paranormal activity in the hotel has been traced to a specific source. A couple who spent the night in suite 2416 reported being terrified one night when the balcony door suddenly flew open. At the same time, the room was filled with an eerie glow. Before the guests had time to react, the door slammed shut, and they were enveloped in darkness.

THE JULIETTE GORDON LOW HOUSE

SAVANNAH

James Moore Wayne, a lawyer, judge and mayor of Savannah, built the Juliette Gordon Low House at the corner of Bull Street and Oglethorpe Avenue between 1818 and 1821. English architect William Jay designed the brick-covered stucco home in the Federal style. Ten years after Wayne and his wife, Elizabeth, moved into the home, Wayne sold it to his niece, Sarah Stiles Gordon, and her husband, William Washington Gordon I. Their son, William Washington Gordon II, and his wife, Eleanor Kinsice Gordon, were the next generation of the Gordon family to occupy the house. "Willie," as William was known, was a successful cotton broker; Eleanor "Nellie" Gordon was a writer. Their second child, Juliette, who achieved fame as the founder of the Girl Scouts, was born in the house on October 31, 1860. Six months later, her father enlisted in the Confederate

The ghosts of Juliette Gordon Low and her husband were seen walking out of the house together on the day she died.

army. During the war, General William Tecumseh Sherman, who was a friend of the family, visited the Gordon home in Savannah several times. William Gordon returned to his home in Savannah after President Andrew Johnson's amnesty proclamation was issued. After William's mother, Sarah, died in the house in 1882, he bought the house to ensure that it remained in the Gordon family. In 1953, the Girl Scouts of America bought the house and assumed stewardship of the property. Over the next three years, the house was restored and furnished with memorabilia from the Gordon family. It opened as a house museum in 1956.

Granted, Juliette Gordon Low had a very strong connection to the family home. However, it is her parents' spirits who are said to remain in the house. William died in 1912. Four years later, Nellie's health began to decline dramatically. Shortly before she died in 1917, Nellie insisted that none of her children "wear mourning." Instead, they should celebrate her death because she would be reunited with her beloved Willie. The story goes that when Nellie died on February 22, 1917, her daughter-in-law, Margaret, saw the ghost of her father-in-law walk into his wife's bedroom as she lay dying. A few minutes later, a family member informed her that Nellie had just passed away. In a quivering voice, Margaret told her and other family members what she had just seen, but no one believed her, except for Juliette. She was walking down the stairs to tell everyone about her mother's death when the family butler assured her that everything would be all right because he had just seen her mother and father walk out the front door, hand in hand.

Some people say that Nellie's ghost is still in the house that she and her husband called home. According to the article "The Ghosts of the Juliette Gordon Low House" on the Ghost City Tours website, Nellie's ghost has been sighted staring out the window and sipping a cup of tea in the dining room. Some visitors claim to have seen Nellie's ghost playing the piano in the living room. A woman who had visited the house as a Girl Scout said that she and her friends brought cameras with them but were told that photography was not allowed inside the house. During the tour, one of the cameras turned off by itself, and the batteries died in another. Needless to say, the girls felt pretty uncomfortable during the remainder of the tour.

THE KEHOE HOUSE

SAVANNAH

The Kehoe House was built in 1842 by William Kehoe, an immigrant from County Wexland, Ireland. He was accompanied by his mother, father, four brothers and three sisters. Kehoe began as an apprentice in an iron foundry located east of Broughton Street. Through hard work and diligence, Kehoe worked his way up to foreman. A few years later, he bought the foundry. In the early 1900s, Kehoe located a new factory on the waterfront. By the end of World War I, William Kehoe had become one of Savannah's most prominent businessmen.

William Kehoe and his wife, Anne Flood, settled down in a home at 130 Habersham Street soon after their marriage in 1868. As his wealth increased, Kehoe decided that he, his wife and their ten children should move to a new home that reflected their lofty social status. In the early 1890s, he hired DeWitt Bruyn to design an imposing mansion in the Queen Anne architectural style. The house was completed in 1802 at 123 Habersham Street at a cost of $25,000. In 1930, William Kehoe's family sold the house. For the next forty-seven years, Goette's Funeral Home occupied the stately mansion. New York Jets football legend Joe Namath owned the Kehoe House until 1990, when it was converted into a bed-and-breakfast. The Kehoe House was sold in 2003; in 2007, HLC Hotels bought it. Today, the William Kehoe House is one of Savannah's finest—and most haunted—bed-and-breakfasts.

The ghosts of children are reported to be the most active spirits inside the William Kehoe House. For many years, people believed they were the ghosts of two of William Kehoe's sons who got themselves trapped in the chimney. The truth is much more mundane but no less tragic. Kehoe's twin daughters, Anne and Mary, died of roseola when they were very young. They are playful little spirits whose spectral giggles, whispers and footsteps have sent shivers up the spines of guests for years. The two little girls seem to delight in tormenting guests by standing at the foot of the bed and staring at them until they wake up. Anne and Mary are also believed to be the entities responsible for turning doorknobs when no one is standing in the hallway. A clerk working at the front desk heard the doorbell ring one morning. His blood pressure rose when he looked through the curtains and saw that no one was standing on the front porch. Some guests have even complained about the unruly children to the night manager, who assures them that adult

Occasionally, guests sleeping at the William Kehoe House are awakened by the playful ghosts of two little girls.

guests are discouraged from bringing their children with them. Other people report feeling unseen fingers touching their arms at night.

William Kehoe's wife, Anne, is also an active presence in the house. She is popularly known as the "Lady in White," whose manifestations are restricted to the second floor, for the most part. Overnight guests claim to have seen her sitting on the corner of the bed. According to a few guests and employees, Anne's ghost has also been seen sitting at her desk on the second floor. Occasionally, Anne's spirit appears on the third floor, where her grandchildren spent a lot of time.

In his book *Haunted Savannah*, author James Caskey tells a frightening tale about a tour guide's strange encounter at the Kehoe House one night.

She was leading her tour group past the Kehoe House when she heard a little boy say, in a pleading voice, "Come play with me." Thinking that she was hearing things, the tour guide continued walking past the house. A few steps later, one of the members of the tour group came up to her and asked if she had heard an eerie little voice. The tour guide just smiled and continued walking.

LAKE LANIER

NORTHERN GEORGIA

By the mid-1940s, the federal government was making plans to dam the Chattahoochee River in northern Georgia. In 1948, the government bought fifty thousand acres at $50 an acre from private individuals and businesses. Between 250 and 700 families were relocated. Six churches and fifteen businesses, mostly wooden structures, were disassembled and rebuilt in different locations. Brick and concrete buildings were left to be submerged in the lake. The bodily remains in twenty cemeteries were exhumed and reburied elsewhere; many people believe, however, that a number of small cemeteries are now under the lake. Construction of the Buford Dam began in 1950 and was completed in 1956 at a cost of $45 million. Not only was the Looper Speedway inundated, but so was an entire town, Oscarville. The human cost of Georgia's largest lake is remembered in the stories people tell about the reservoir.

Since the lake opened in 1956, approximately 675 people have died on it in various ways. A number of boats have capsized after striking something unseen in the water. Cars have slid off the embankment into the lake. Drownings are common in the lake as well. A number of the drowning victims were said to be strong swimmers. The fact that some of the bodies were never recovered has fostered rumors that the lake is bottomless. The death toll is so high, in fact, that many people believe that Lake Lanier is cursed. Some divers claim to have felt an immobile arm or leg in the murky darkness of the lake. Swimmers who have barely escaped drowning claim that it felt like someone was pulling them under the water.

A lake with a history as dark as Lake Lanier's is bound to generate ghost stories. Lake Lanier's best-known ghost story was spawned by an accident that occurred in 1958. Delia Mae Parker Young was driving her 1954 Ford

Since its completion in 1956, Lake Lanier has had an unusually high death toll, leading some to believe that it is cursed. *Wikimedia Commons.*

with a friend, Susie Roberts, to a roadhouse in Dawsonville, Georgia. While crossing the Lanier Bridge, Susie ran her car off the bridge's right abutment. Because of the skid marks leading into the water, divers searched the lake but found nothing. The human remains that floated to the surface of the lake the next year only added to the mystery. Because the corpse's hands were missing, identifying the corpse was impossible. Authorities assumed that the skeleton belonged to one of the women, but they were not entirely certain.

In 1990, the mystery of the fate of the two women was solved with the discovery of Susie Roberts's 1954 Ford while the lake was being dredged. The skeleton sitting behind the wheel was positively identified as being that of Susie Roberts through her purse, ring and watch. The remains discovered in 1959 were finally determined to be those of Delia Mae Parker Young. Her spirit is assumed to be the ghostly Lady in Blue that has been sighted walking on Lanier Bridge for decades, because it is missing both hands.

The Lady in Blue is not Lake Lanier's only ghost. According to the website Southern Gothic Media, one night at 1:00 a.m., two fishermen witnessed someone trying to keep his raft afloat. Suddenly, the man screamed and plunged into the frigid water. The two fishermen went ashore and shined their lantern on the spot where the man jumped into the water but saw neither him nor his raft.

Some government officials have disagreed with the claim that Lake Lanier is cursed. In 2017, a representative of the Department of Natural Resources said that the high number of deaths in Lake Lanier can be credited to its large number of visitors. However, according to the *Atlanta Journal-Constitution*, Lake Lanier's mortality rate was twice that of the state's second-largest lake, which, in 2017, was only 7 percent smaller in popularity.

The Marshall House Hotel

SAVANNAH

Mary Marshall built the Marshall House Hotel at 123 East Broughton Street in 1851. The distinctive cast-iron veranda and balconies were added in 1857. The Marshall House doubled as a field hospital twice in its history. The Union army, under the command of General William Tecumseh Sherman, occupied the hotel from 1864 to 1865. It was used to treat wounded soldiers until the end of the war. Later, the City of Savannah requisitioned it as a place where victims of two of its yellow fever epidemics could be treated. Even the fire department used the hotel for a brief time in 1867. The guest list of the old hotel is impressive, including author Joel Chandler Harris during Reconstruction. Minnie Geiger took control of the hotel around the turn of the century and renamed it the Geiger Hotel. Herbert W. Gilbert leased the hotel from 1933 to 1945, when it closed. The hotel reopened in 1946 as the Marshall Hotel. In 1957, the second, third and fourth floors were closed; shops were housed on the first floor. The hotel reopened in 1999 under a new name—the Marshall House Hotel—following a $12 million renovation. In 2014, the guest rooms and suites were completely renovated. Six years later, the library and lobby were renovated as well.

The eyewitness accounts from staff and guests suggest that not all of the occupants of the rooms in the Marshall House are among the living. For example, the building's Civil War past reveals itself in unexpected moments. In rooms 214, 314 and 414, guests have been awakened by the nauseating odor of rotting flesh. This phenomenon could be related to a

Built in 1851, the Marshall House Hotel was converted into a hospital during the Civil War and Savannah's yellow fever epidemic of 1876.

discovery made in the 1990s when the hotel was being remodeled. Workers removing the floorboards in a downstairs office found piles of amputated bones. Not surprisingly, this office was used as an operating room in the winter of 1864. The ghostly forms of Union soldiers have been sighted in this room as well. No one knows why the putrid smell centers on these rooms.

The makeshift hospital that was set up for yellow fever victims inside the Marshall House reasserts itself occasionally as well. Because many of the patients who died here were children, much of the paranormal activity in the hotel suggests that their spirits are manifesting themselves through their childish laughter. The crying of babies and the sounds of bouncing balls and rolling marbles have been reported as well. A few guests claim to have seen the ghosts of small children running and playing in the hallways.

The personal identity of one of the hotel's spirits could have something to do with the way in which it makes its presence known. For years, people have heard the clattering of an old typewriter coming from the room once occupied by Joel Chandler Harris, the author of the Uncle Remus

Over the years, guests at the Marshall House have been startled by the sudden appearance of Union soldiers and a putrid odor coming from rooms 214, 314 and 414.

stories. Some guests and employees believe that he could be the gentleman dressed in a nineteenth-century suit who has been sighted reading a book by the window.

Some of the evidence of hauntings inside the hotel cannot be traced to a single specific source. Faucets have been known to turn on by themselves in some of the rooms. Guests have been awakened by the sound of someone turning the doorknob to their room. On the fourth floor, guests have heard a loud crashing sound early in the morning. When my wife, Marilyn, and I stayed in a room on the fourth floor on July 24, 2001, I was awakened at 2:00 a.m. by a thumping sound on the door. Hoping to make a personal connection with one of the hotel's legendary phantoms, I jumped out of bed and opened the door. I was disappointed when I did not see Casper standing there, but when I went to bed, I realized that the thumping sound might have been his way of saying hello.

THE MOON RIVER BREWING COMPANY

SAVANNAH

The building that houses the Moon River Brewing Company was built in 1821 as the City Hotel by Eleazer Early, who hoped that it would attract wealthy guests looking for a luxurious getaway. Indeed, the City Hotel was popular with a number of famous guests, including painter John James Audubon. Just before General William Tecumseh Sherman's forces took possession of Savannah in 1864, the City Hotel closed. During the remainder of the nineteenth century, the former hotel was used as a hospital several times during Savannah's yellow fever epidemics.

The former hotel's violent past seems to have made a lasting psychic imprint on the second floor. In 1832, Dr. Phillip Minus became involved in a disagreement with a drunken troublemaker named James Stark. As tempers flared, the argument escalated into a shouting match, which ended when Dr. Minus pulled out his pistol and shot Stark. The doctor's claim that he killed Stark as he was reaching for his gun, along with Stark's bad reputation, convinced the authorities to drop the charges. A second violent

Built by Eleazer Early as the City Hotel in 1821, the building served a number of purposes before becoming the Moon River Brewing Company in 1995.

event took place in the hotel twenty-eight years later, just before the outbreak of the Civil War. A Northerner named James Sinclair booked a room in the hotel. Outraged by the presence of a Yankee in Savannah, a group of citizens approached him in the hotel and pleaded with him to leave. When he refused, an angry mob took him by force outside the hotel and gave him a severe beating.

Many people believe that the spirits of all the people who died at the Moon River Brewing Company are making life for the employees and patrons interesting, to say the least. People on ghost tours claim to have had some sort of weird experience here. According to the website moonriverbrewing. com, the upper floors are unfinished because the spirits have scared off the workers. Many of these ghosts could possibly be the spirits of the hundreds of children who died here in the yellow fever epidemics.

The Moon River Brewing Company's most famous ghost is an apparition known only as Toby, the spirit that haunts the basement. He has been sighted walking in the shadowy recesses of the basement. People playing pool in the basement have reported that an invisible presence brushed against them, ruining their shot. Others have walked into cold spots throughout the basement. One guest even felt icy fingers touching her neck when she was

Guests venturing into the basement have encountered a "cold spirit" named Toby.

Guests eating in the dining room have had their meals interrupted by overly friendly spirits.

the only one present. This same entity is probably the one throwing bottles across the basement floor in an attempt to get attention.

The main floor where the dining room is located has also had its share of paranormal activity, probably because this is the floor where Dr. Minus shot James Stark. Women walking into the ladies' room have been overcome with a feeling of intense coldness. A few have even been locked in the stalls when no one else was present. A female patron jumped up from her seat one night when something grabbed her leg twice. She knew that her date had not touched her because both of his hands were clearly visible on the tabletop.

The third and fourth floors are the most haunted parts of the Moon River Brewing Company. A "woman in white," also referred to as Mrs. Johnson, walks the halls of the third floor. Because this is the floor where young victims of the yellow fever epidemics were treated, staff and patrons have heard ghostly children laughing, talking and running down the hallways. A much more aggressive ghost has even pushed people down the stairs on the third floor. The spectral voices of children have also been heard on the top floor, where even more yellow fever victims were treated. Reports such as these explain why the Moon River Brewing Company has been called one of the most haunted places in the United States.

The Morton Theatre

ATHENS

Monroe Bowers Morton built the Morton Theatre in 1910. The theater is noteworthy because it is one of the few existing vaudeville theaters in the nation that was managed and owned by an African American person. A number of well-known African Americans performed here, such as Bessie Smith and Cab Calloway. Later on, movies were shown at the theater. The building also provided office space for Black professionals, such as doctors, pharmacists and dentists. The Morton Theatre has been restored and is now in the National Register of Historic Places.

As far as haunted theaters go, the Morton Theatre is somewhat typical in that it is haunted by the ghosts of former employees. It stands out from the rest, however, in that these employees were children who moved props backstage for vaudeville acts. In an article published in *The Red and Black* by Kyra Posey, a local historian named Jeff Clarke said that one of the staff members who had brought his daughter to the theater noticed that she was speaking to another girl on the stage. After a few minutes, he asked her about her little friend. She replied that the girl had vanished while she was talking to her.

Acclaimed as one of the few remaining vaudeville theaters owned and operated by an African American, the Morton Theatre is said to be haunted by the ghosts of children who once worked there.

Further evidence of haunted activity was proved by an all-night visit to the theater on October 11, 2014, by Ghosts of Georgia paranormal investigators. During the night, two of the members heard a ghostly voice say "Hey, hey, hey!" They also saw a number of green lights flashing along the stage. Another member saw a shadow figure move across the stage and heard a chain-like rattle on the catwalk. Disembodied voices were heard coming from the dressing room. Clearly, the spirits of the Morton Theatre were treating the investigators to a private performance that night.

THE OLDE PINK HOUSE

SAVANNAH

The Olde Pink House in Savannah, Georgia, has a history that parallels that of the early United States. It was built by James Habersham Jr. between 1771 and 1779 on land granted by the Crown of England. James and his two brothers were members of the Sons of Liberty, despite the fact that their father was a Loyalist. The three brothers held secret meetings in the house to free Georgia and the other colonies from British rule. During the Revolutionary War, British soldiers were housed within James's house. All three brothers fought in the Revolutionary War. James finished building his home after the war ended using red brick. The red color bled through the plaster that was used to cover the house, turning it pink. In 1811, the house became the Planter's Bank. It survived the War of 1812 and the Great Savannah Fire of 1820. During the Civil War, one of William Tecumseh Sherman's generals, General York, used the Olde Pink House as

The three sons of James Habersham Sr. held clandestine meetings of the Sons of Liberty inside the Olde Pink House during the Revolutionary War.

his headquarters. After the Civil War, the Olde Pink House was used as a lawyer's office, a bookstore and a colonial tearoom before being restored and converted into a restaurant in 1992.

The ghost stories that focus on the Olde Pink House reflect its long history. For years, patrons claim to have seen a Revolutionary War soldier sitting at the bar, drinking. Some claim that he made a toast with them before disappearing. The ghosts of slave children who may have died in the fire in 1820 or in one of the city's yellow fever epidemics have been known to play tricks on patrons. They may be the spirits responsible for locking women inside the bathroom. Workers closing up the restaurant one evening heard the spectral weeping of a woman. The restaurant's most famous apparition is the ghost of James Habersham Jr., who, history tells us, died of natural causes within the house and was buried with the rest of his family in Colonial Cemetery in Savannah. According to local legend, however, James became despondent upon discovering that his wife had a lover and killed himself in the basement. It is important to note that no historical evidence exists supporting this story. The legend explains why his ghost has been sighted primarily in the basement, which also serves as the tavern for the restaurant. Staff members say he is a fastidious spirit who straightens up tablecloths and relights candles while they are closing up for the night. Security cameras may have captured one of the ghosts in 2011. Camera footage shows a hazy figure floating down a hallway and then disappearing.

ORNA VILLA

OXFORD

Richard K. Dearing built the Greek Revival house known as Orna Villa on Emory Street in 1825. Five years later, Dr. Alexander Means purchased the house. He was a member of the original faculty of Emory University and served as its president for a year. As a pioneering natural scientist, he became fascinated with electricity. In 1858, Dr. Means displayed a functional incandescent bulb to a group of Atlanta citizens. His interests also extended to the fields of chemistry, botany, physics and theology. He spent hours reading and rocking in his rocking chair in his bedroom to keep from falling asleep.

Dr. Means's love of reading and learning was not passed down to his son Tobe, who hated books and had no desire to pursue a career path similar

The restless spirits of Dr. Means's two sons, Tobe and Owen, disturb the peace at Orna Villa. *Wikimedia Commons.*

to his father's. Instead, Tobe preferred to experience the world firsthand through traveling. His father always flew into a rage when Tobe asked him for the money he had set aside for his education so that he could use it to "see the world." These arguments over Tobe's refusal to go to college went on for several months. The rift between father and son became even wider one night after a particularly vocal altercation. After a few minutes, Tobe stomped out of his father's study and began pacing back and forth on the back porch. Sometime later, Tobe rode away on his horse. He never returned.

Not all of Dr. Means's nine children refused their father's offer of a college education. Because attending medical school was always a boyhood dream of his son Olin, he threw himself, body and soul, into becoming a first-rate physician. Over time, however, his mild interest in religion morphed into a burning obsession. One evening, Olin walked into his father's study and confessed that he was torn between practicing medicine and preaching the Gospel. Dr. Means listened intently to his son's dilemma and then advised him to make up his own mind. Olin shook his father's hand, walked out of his office and began pacing back and forth on the back porch while wrestling with the most difficult decision of his life. While Olin was trying to choose between the two equally respectable careers, his father took ill and died, never learning of his son's decision.

In her book *Georgia Ghosts and Jeffrey*, author Kathryn Tucker Windham wrote about the hauntings of Orna Villa. For about a century, the most persistent and tantalizing evidence of ghosts has been the phantom footsteps on the back porch at night. Those familiar with the history of the Means family have traced the source of the ghostly pacing to two of Dr. Means's sons, Tobe and Olin. According to Windham, one of the owners, E.H. Rheberg, woke up early one morning to go over the plans for renovating the old house when he heard someone walking on the back porch. He assumed that one of the carpenters he had hired was waiting to be let in. Rheberg expected to see one of the men standing there when he unlatched the door, but no one was there.

By the 1970s, the back porch had been enclosed, putting an end to the constant walking in the dark. However, the restless spirits of Tobe and Olin Means announced their presence in other ways. Pictures fell off the walls for no apparent reason. Antique guns that were anchored to the wall by means of brackets fell to the floor one night, barely missing the glass-front bookcase underneath. A birdcage that was hung from a nail fell down as well. Owners have also heard the regular rocking of a rocking chair in Dr. Means's former study.

The history of Orna Villa did not end with the Means family. During the Civil War, it was used as a field hospital. In 1973, Orna Villa was listed in the National Register of Historic Places. In the television series *The Vampire Diaries* (2009–17), the historic home was transformed into a fraternity house for a party scene. Today, Orna Villa is one of the most lovingly restored homes in Oxford's historic district.

THE OWENS-THOMAS HOUSE

SAVANNAH

Designed by English architect William Jay for wealthy cotton merchant Richard Richardson, the Owens-Thomas House was built between 1816 and 1819 at 124 Abercorn Street in Savannah. The house was noteworthy for its indoor plumbing, which was a rarity at that time. Richardson had not lived in his home for very long before the Great Fire of 1820 consumed more than four hundred homes and business. That same year, a yellow fever epidemic claimed hundreds of lives. Between 1820 and 1828, the house was converted

"The Lady in Gray" has been sighted walking through the courtyard of the Owen-Thomas House at sunset.

into a boardinghouse run by Mary Maxwell. Its most famous occupant, the Marquis de Lafayette, gave a speech from the balcony of the south side of the house during his visit in 1825. After George Welshman Owens, a former mayor of Savannah, bought the house in 1830 for $10,000, it remained in his family until 1951, when his granddaughter Margaret Thomas donated it to the Telfair Museum of Art. The Owens-Thomas House is now open to the public as a house museum. Not only does the Owens-Thomas House boast the earliest example of indoor plumbing in Savannah and the most intact slave quarters open to the public in Savannah, but it also has some fascinating paranormal activity.

Margaret Thomas may have bestowed her house to the Telfair Museum of Art, but some say that she remains in the house in spirit. "The Lady in Gray," as she has come to be known, was in the habit of walking through the courtyard wearing a gray shawl and a large hat. Her ghost is usually sighted strolling through the courtyard around dusk. Interestingly enough, she was often mistaken for a ghost when she was alive, possibly because she was in the habit of wearing a long, old-fashioned gown.

A male ghost has been sighted in the Owens-Thomas House as well. In the 1960s, John Berendt, the author of *Midnight in the Garden of Good and Evil*, was visiting his business partner and a friend, who was renting out the entire third floor of the house. John and his business partner were sitting in chairs facing their host, who was sitting on a two-seat couch. The three were talking when they suddenly noticed a man wearing a riding shirt, black boots and a shirt with ruffles in the room behind the couch. John said that the man walked through the couch and stood over him. He was so close that he could see beads of sweat on the equestrian's forehead. His business partner, who was visibly shaken, also saw the apparition

In her book *Savannah Spectres and Other Strange Tales*, author Margaret Wayt DeBolt told the story of a maid who locked up the house one day and went home. When she returned the next morning, she was surprised to find that one of the chairs had been pulled out from the antique dining table, as if someone had sat down to a meal. Not long thereafter, the same maid discovered a puddle of water on the floor. The spot was several feet away from any windows or plumbing.

Originally, the slave quarters were located in the carriage house. The ceiling of the carriage house is painted a bright blue color called "haint blue." It was made with a combination of indigo dye, milk and lime. Supposedly, the blue color represented the colors of bodies of water, like lakes and ponds. Because spirits cannot cross water, they avoided any houses painted this color. Ironically, though, some guests have felt uneasy in the carriage house after dark.

THE PIRATE'S HOUSE

SAVANNAH

Built in 1753, the Pirate's House is the oldest building in the city. It originally served as an inn and tavern. Meals were served on the first floor; guests spent the night in the beds on the second floor. Counted among its customers were sailors, merchant marines, French and English privateers and other assorted scoundrels. Impressment, or shanghaiing, was a common practice until 1811. Sea captains in need of a crew singled out likely candidates at the bar and plied them with drinks. Their victims were then taken down to a brick tunnel in the basement that led to the seafront, where the men were loaded onto the waiting ships. In the 1920s, a jazz bar called Hard-Hearted Hannah's

Alcoholic spirits mingle with the spirits of some of the Pirate's House's more unsavory former guests to create a unique dining experience.

was housed in the upstairs rooms. By World War II, the dilapidated building was practically abandoned. Just before the building was scheduled to be demolished, it was purchased by the Savannah Gas Company in 1945. Mary Hillyer, the wife of the president of the gas company, and other women in the community oversaw the restoration of the historic inn. Today, the Pirate's House is one of Savannah's most unique restaurants.

The Pirate's House's legacy extends well beyond its history as a hangout for buccaneers and cutthroats. Author Robert Louis Stevenson was inspired to write his 1883 novel *Treasure Island* following his visit to the Savannah inn. Today, fans of the paranormal consider the Pirate's House one of Savannah's haunted hot spots. Before the brick tunnels were closed at both ends, workers reported hearing moans, voices and yelling coming from somewhere down below. Inside the dining room, patrons and work staff have heard the stomping of heavy, leather-soled boots on the wooden floors. A scar-faced sailor makes occasional appearances in the basement and on the second floor. One night, a coffeepot flew across the room as if it was thrown by invisible hands. One of the most haunted parts of the Pirate's House is the cellar beneath the Captain's Room, where spectral voices resound in the dark recesses. History, it seems, cannot be confined to the past in the Pirate's House.

Sibley Mill

AUGUSTA

After the seven-mile Augusta Canal was dug in 1845, Augusta was transformed into a major industrial site. In 1861, Major Charles Shaler Smith constructed the Confederate Powder Works in Augusta. Consisting of twenty-six buildings, the complex became the second-largest gunpowder factory in the world. Even though part of the factory was destroyed by a violent explosion in 1864, the production of gunpowder continued until 1865. After the war, the federal government took it over and eventually sold the property. The buildings were razed to make room for the widening of the canal. In 1878, the Enterprise Mill was erected on the site of the powder works with bricks from the demolished factory. Two years later, Sibley Manufacturing received a charter to operate on the site. The 528-foot-long factory contained twenty-four thousand spindles for the production of textiles. The Graniteville Company purchased the textile mill in 1940. In the late 1970s, the Levi Strauss Company began making denim on the site.

Built in 1878 on the site of the Confederate Powder Works, the Sibley Mill is rumored to house the ghost of a woman who was murdered by a co-worker after she broke up with him.

Operations inside the old mill were curtailed in 2006. Most of the equipment inside the building was removed.

According to the website Haunted Rooms America, most of the haunted activity inside the old mill can be traced to a violent incident that occurred in 1906. At this time, a married millworker named Arthur Glover was having an affair with a co-worker named Maude Williams. After Maude broke up with Glover, he burst into the mill on October 20 and shot her. Maude's apparition has been seen many times in the weaving room. Her appearance is so lifelike that new employees have tried to strike up a conversation with her before she fades away.

THE ST. SIMONS LIGHTHOUSE

ST. SIMONS ISLAND

Built in 1810, the original lighthouse on St. Simons Island was destroyed by Confederate soldiers fleeing the approaching Union army. The U.S. government replaced the first light tower with a 104-foot structure. Its third-order biconvex Fresnel lens projects four beams of light. In 1934, a one-thousand-watt electrical light was installed, replacing the kerosene-burning lamp. The U.S. Coast Guard assumed ownership of the lighthouse on July 1, 1939. The lighthouse keeper's cottage was restored by the Georgia Historical Society between 1972 and 1975. The lighthouse tower was restored three times: 1989–91, 1997–98 and 2010. It is now under the control of the Georgia Historical Society. Not only is the St. Simons Lighthouse one of five light towers remaining in Georgia, but it is also one of the most haunted.

The ghost haunting the St. Simons Lighthouse is believed to be the spirit of Frederick Osborne, who replaced the first lighthouse keeper, Bradford B. Brunt, in 1874. The date of his birth is uncertain. He was probably born in England in 1841 or 1843. Osborne arrived in New York on April 1, 1863. He enlisted in the Union army on April 27, 1863. He served in Battery K, Fourth New York. After the Civil War, he served in the Southwest with the regular United States Army. In 1867, Osborne was mustered out of the army at Fort Union. Sometime after 1870, he married Julia Pauline-Pagson. In 1873, he became a naturalized U.S. citizen. Shortly thereafter, he moved to South Carolina, where he worked at the Cape Romain Lighthouse. His

The ghost of the first lighthouse keeper, Frederick Osborne, is said to haunt the St. Simons Lighthouse. *Wikimedia Commons.*

wife gave birth to a son, William Thomas Osborne, on November 5, 1873. The next year, Frederick began working at the St. Simons Lighthouse on St. Simons Island. The couple's second son, Frederick Page Osborne, was born on October 19, 1875, but died two years later. Their third child, Elizabeth Frederick Osborne, was born on February 14, 1880. Osborne and his family lived on the first floor of the brick cottage at the base of the lighthouse. His assistant, John W. Stephens, and his wife moved into the second floor of the cottage in 1880. A central stairway connected the two floors.

In March 1880, the relationship between the two men came to a violent end. In one of the variants of the story, Osborne flirted with Mrs. Stephens while her husband was gone. In another version of the tale, Osborne criticized Mrs. Stephens for not keeping her part of the cottage clean. According to an article that appeared in the *Brunswick Advertiser* on March 6, 1880, an argument that had been slowly growing for several days finally came to a head one Sunday morning at 8:30 a.m. in the bushes outside the cottage. Stephens threatened to beat up Osborne, who drew a pistol on his assistant and warned him not to come any closer. Stephens ran back inside the cottage and got his double-barrel shotgun, loaded with birdshot for deer hunting. As Osborne was walking along a path toward the cottage, Stephens fired once from the front of the cottage, hitting Osborne in four places. Shaken by what he had done, Stephens took Osborne to the hospital in Brunswick, where he passed away, despite the best efforts of the island physician and the mainland physician. The authorities arrested Stephens and charged him with murder. However, by trial's end, the jury had acquitted Stephens of all charges.

Not long after the shooting, newspapers began publishing stories about Osborne's restless spirit at the lighthouse. One of the most famous accounts, published in a newspaper in 1908, concerned Annie Svendsen, the wife of lighthouse keeper Carl Svendsen. One dark, windy night when her husband was gone, she was having problems with the mechanism of the light. As she was trying to fix it, she recalled Frederick Osborne's promise to help her with the light if she was unable to take care of the problem herself. In frustration, she called out, "Well, come and fix it now!" Suddenly, she beheld the figure of Frederick Osborne peering into the machinery. Overcome with shock and fear, she fainted dead away. When she regained consciousness, the machinery was working perfectly.

In her book *Georgia Ghosts*, author Nancy Roberts said that John Stephens was never the same following the death of his friend. He became a skittish man who reported hearing strange sounds in his room. Friends of Stephens got into the habit of announcing their presence before knocking on the door to avoid "scaring him to death." Stephens told one of his friends that on dark, stormy nights, when he was alone at the top tower, he heard the *clomp, clomp, clomp* of heavy boots climbing the stairs. The disembodied footsteps always stopped when they reached Stephens's platform. It is no small wonder that several years ago, *Coastal Magazine* listed the St. Simons Lighthouse as number four in its list of the Top 15 Haunted Lighthouses.

TELFAIR ACADEMY

SAVANNAH

In 1819, a wealthy resident of Savannah named Alexander Telfair hired English architect William Jay to design a mansion in the Neoclassical Regency style. Jay went on to design four other "little palaces" in Savannah.

The Telfair Mansion was built on the site of the former colonial Government House. Following the death of the heir to the family fortune, Alexander's sister, Mary, in 1875, the mansion was bequeathed in her will to the Georgia Historical Society, which hired Carl Brandt to remodel the house and build an addition where a new collection of art would be displayed. One of the attendees for the formal opening of the museum in 1886 was former president of the Confederacy Jefferson Davis. Not only is Telfair Academy the oldest museum in the southern region, but it is also the first museum in the United States to be founded by a woman.

Over the years, staff members have learned that disregarding Mary Telfair's wishes in her will has serious consequences. In her will, Mary stipulated that "no eating, drinking, smoking, or amusements of any kind" were allowed inside the museum. In her book *Savannah Specters and Other Tales*, author Margaret Wayt DeBolt includes a strange incident that occurred one day when the Georgia Historical Society held its meeting on the museum's lawn. All at once, dark clouds blotted out the sun; rain and hail soon followed, forcing the guests and staff to take shelter inside. Tables and refreshments were carried inside as well. The guests were trying to dry off when a gust of wind blew through the building, causing a glass to fall off a table and break. Rather than risk Mary Telfair's disapproval again, the administrators decided to serve refreshments only in the annex.

The vigilant spirit of Mary Telfair makes her presence known at the Telfair Museum when the rules stipulated in her will are not followed.

The staff inadvertently incurred Mary Telfair's wrath on another occasion as well. Even though Mary Telfair never said that her huge portrait must remain in its original location in the dining room, staff members have always believed that this is where she wanted it. Their assumption was confirmed one day in the mid-1980s when workmen moved her portrait. Suddenly, part of the rotunda fell through the lower ceiling beneath it.

Over the years, other reports of paranormal activity inside the museum have surfaced. Spectral harp music has been known to waft through the museum on occasion. Visitors have also heard the sound of spectral footsteps. Pounding vibrations of unknown origin have set off burglar alarms. Doors open on their own. In an article appearing in the *Sun-Sentinel*, Barbara Fultz, a tour guide with Tours by BJ, told reporter Carolyn Thornton that late one afternoon, she was trying to round up all forty-two people from a motor coach tour who were inside the museum. "I gathered the ones I could find, but two were missing," Fultz said. "I was standing at the stairs, looking for them, and it was as if someone said, 'Barbara, look around.' I turned and saw the leg of a woman with a big top button shoe and long dress disappear around the door."

William Root House

MARIETTA

William Root built his house at the intersection of Church and Lemon Streets. After the house was enlarged in the 1890s, it was moved down Lemon Street. In 1990, the house was moved to Polk Street and the 120 Loop. Just before the city planned to demolish the historic house, it was donated to the Landmarks and Historical Society. The detached kitchen was restored to its nineteenth-century appearance.

William Root is remembered today as Marietta's first druggist. While living in the house, he and his wife, the former Hannah Simpson, had four children. As one of the city's most prominent citizens, Root became one of the founders of St. James Episcopal Church. Following the death of one of his sons and the failure of his pharmacy, Root found employment at the church. Beginning in 1883, Root served as the county coroner for two years. He died in 1891.

Halloween preparations may have made it easier for visitors to the William Root House to see the ghosts of the pharmacist's wife and young son. *Wikimedia Commons.*

Like many historic homes in Georgia, the William Root House is said to be haunted by the spirits of its former occupants. Legend has it that the ghosts of Hannah Root and her young son still walk the halls of the pharmacist's house. Some locals and visitors claim to have seen Hannah's ghost staring out of bedroom windows on the second floor. Docents who open the house museum in the morning have found evidence that the rope bed has been slept in, even though no one was in the house. Of course, the imaginations of visitors may be fueled by the fact that in the month of October, a coffin is on display in the parlor and the mirrors and pictures are draped in black crepe, just as they would have been during a nineteenth-century funeral.

THE WREN'S NEST

ATLANTA

Joel Chandler Harris was born in Eatonton on December 9, 1845. After his father deserted his mother, Harris and his mother lived in a cottage behind Dr. Andrew Reid's mansion. His mother supported herself and her son by gardening and sewing for neighbors. Dr. Reid paid for Harris's education at the Eatonton Academy, where he developed a love for reading. At that time, Harris had red hair and a stammer. He was also small for his age. In 1862, Harris was employed as a printing compositor for Joseph Addison Turner at his Turnworld Plantation. Harris first heard the oral tales of Br'er Rabbit and other animals while working for Turner. After Turner's newspaper closed in 1866, Harris worked at a variety of publications over the next ten years. When a yellow fever epidemic drove him and his family out of Savannah in 1876, they relocated to Atlanta, where he found work at the *Atlanta Constitution*. According to legend, Harris began writing the Uncle Remus stories while filling in for a column writer. Set on an antebellum plantation, the stories were told by a fictional African American slave created by Harris. In 1880, he compiled the Uncle Remus stories from his newspaper columns into a book titled *Uncle Remus: His Songs and His Sayings—The Folklore of the Old Plantation*. The book was so popular that it earned Harris a national reputation.

In 1885, Harris moved his family into a one-story farmhouse at 21 Gordon Street, just southwest of Atlanta. George Muse had built the farmhouse on

Joel Chandler Harris moved his family into a farmhouse he called the Wren's Nest.

a five-acre tract in 1870. Over time, the address was changed to 1050 Ralph David Abernathy Boulevard. After a wren built a nest in the mailbox, Harris changed the name of the house to the Wren's Nest. The children persuaded Harris to build another mailbox so that the wrens could have the original mailbox. Harris hired architect George P. Humphreys to remodel the house. An office on the second floor was intended to serve as Harris's study, but he wrote on the front porch or his bedroom instead. Eventually, Harris and his wife converted the second-floor room into a space for their six children. Following Harris's death in 1908, part of the property was sold. Five years after Harris's death, the Wren's Nest was converted into a museum. Today, the Wren's Nest encompasses three acres. It was designated a National Historic Landmark in 1962. Today, the Queen Anne–style home is the oldest house museum in Atlanta.

Reports of paranormal activity in the Wren's Nest surfaced in the early 2000s. Executive director Melissa Swindle confirmed that Harris's spirit appears to have a strong attachment to at least one of the objects in the house. She reported that after Harris's antique typewriter was loaned out to an old building on Auburn Avenue, the engine in her car refused to turn on in the drive of the Wren's Nest. She speculated, humorously, that this might have been Harris's way of objecting to having his beloved typewriter relocated.

For years, guests walking through the Wren's Nest have reported feeling the presence of spirits. Some of them believe they have actually seen apparitions in the house. Although none of the ghosts has been positively identified, some people are certain that the slim young man in an old-fashioned suit who appears in Harris's bedroom might be the spirit of Harris's son Evelyn. The best-known ghosts, however, are the ghosts of two boys, between three and five years old, whom guests have seen in the yard or on the stairs. According to the website Creative Loathing, they could be the spirits of Harris's grandsons Pierre and Charles, who died in the house. A female apparition who has been sighted watching paranormal investigators could be the ghost of a woman named Chloe who worked at the house.

Evidence of spirits residing in the house museum was collected in a monthlong investigation conducted by the Southeastern Institute of Paranormal Research using EMF meters, infrared cameras and digital voice recorders in February 2019. During the four-part investigation, members of the group recorded voices, some of which were garbled, although a few sentences, such as "That's crazy!," were clear. The investigators also captured a banging sound on their recorders. One night, the founder of

The ghosts of Harris's sons Evelyn and Julian have appeared in Harris's bedroom.

the paranormal group, Denise Roffe, saw a man standing in front of the fireplace in Harris's bedroom. Afterward, she examined photographs of Harris's children. She looked at several pictures before seeing a familiar face. The man she had seen was Julian Harris, a journalist who assisted his father with the publication of the *Uncle Remus Magazine* in early 1907.

Swindle stated on creativeloathing.com that the ghost stories people tell about the Wren's Nest help make history "come alive." She insists that the ghosts, if they exist, do not seem to be malicious: "When the Southeastern Institute of Paranormal Research came in and said there were ghosts, I just figured, well, they aren't bothering me, so I guess we'll be all right."

WRIGHT SQUARE

SAVANNAH

Named after John, Lord Viscount Percival, Earl of Egmont, Percival Square was laid out in 1733. Thirty years later, the city changed the name to Wright

Square. It was named after the last royal governor of Georgia, Sir James Wright. In 1739, a Yamacraw chief, Tomo-Chi-Chi, was given the honor of being buried in the center of the square under a stone pyramid because he had made peace with the Georgia settlers. In 1842, a local politician and wealthy businessman named William Washington Gordon had his memorial erected in Wright Square. However, to make room for it, Chief Tomo-Chi-Chi's pyramid was removed, and according to legend, his bones were strewn over the square. After Gordon's memorial was finished, Tomo-Chi-Chi's new monument was built on the southeastern corner of Wright Square. According to the website ghostcitytours.com, visitors to Wright Square can conjure up the chief's spirit by chanting "Tomo-Chi-Chi" three times.

Wright Square's most famous ghost is the spirit of Alice Riley. In December 1733, Alice and her husband, Richard Wright, were among thirty-eight other indentured Irish servants who arrived in Savannah. Two months later, they were sent to work for William Wise, who owned a cattle farm on Hutchinson Island. A harsh, abusive master, he required that they bathe and groom him daily. Rumors soon spread in the community that

Locals blame the fact that no Spanish moss hangs from the trees in Wright Square on Alice Riley's hanging on January 19, 1795.

he raped Alice as well. After a few months, the couple decided to end their servitude to this brutal man. On March 1, 1734, while they were grooming Wise, Richard shoved Wise's head into a bucket of water after strangling him with a handkerchief. He held his master's head in the bucket for two or three minutes until his struggles finally ceased. They dumped his corpse in the Savannah River, but his body was discovered shortly thereafter. Alice and Richard were immediately designated the prime suspects. The pair fled to the Isle of Hope, where they were taken into custody by the authorities.

After a brief trial, both Alice and Richard were sentenced to death. Richard was the first to hang. Before Alice's sentence could be carried out, she announced in court that she was innocent—and pregnant. The judge agreed to wait until Alice gave birth before hanging her. When her son, James, was born eight months later, the baby was taken from her arms, and she was hanged on January 19, 1735, at Wright Square, also known as the "hanging square." Alice's mournful apparition has been sighted many times at Wright Square, mostly by mothers and pregnant women. Many people believe she is searching for the baby whom she was allowed to hold for only a few minutes. Some locals say that no Spanish moss hangs from the trees on Wright Square because of the legend that nothing ever grows in places where innocent blood has been spilled.

LEGENDARY WOMEN

The Georgia Wonder: Lulu Hurst

CEDARTOWN

Lulu Hurst was born in Collard Valley in 1869. Her mother was a graduate of Mary Sharp College, and her father was known locally as a hero of the Confederacy. When Lulu was a child, she and her family moved to nearby Cedartown. She claimed that on September 18, 1883, she was sleeping with her cousin Lora during a thunderstorm when suddenly, she heard a faint popping sound that began under her pillow and moved throughout the room. The next night, Lulu heard the strange noise once again. This time, she felt as if something was tugging on her hair. Over the next few days, Lulu discovered that she had acquired special powers, such as the ability to make hickory nuts fly through the air and make her clothes move from drawers to cabinets.

When she was sixteen, Lulu learned how to perform acts of great strength. Her neighbors flocked to her house to watch Lulu cause an umbrella to fly apart. In 1884, Lulu hired a manager, Paul M. Atkinson, who booked her at places like the DeGive's Opera House in Atlanta. To prepare for her new career, Lulu bought a black velvet dress and a gold necklace. "The Lulu Show" became an overnight success. Men who held on to one end of a cane found that they were unable to stop her from pulling them around when she was holding on to the curved handle. She astounded audiences by lifting a chair on which three men were sitting. After performing in Chattanooga, Lulu toured Georgia for four months. The *Augusta Chronicle and Sentinel* called the five-foot, six-and-a-half-inch girl "the amazing wonder of the nineteenth century."

During her two-year career, Lulu was interviewed by a number of prominent men who were eager to uncover the source of her power. On one occasion, she was examined by Dr. Alexander Graham Bell, astronomer and inventor William Harkness and geologist John Wesley Powell. The men stood in amazement as they watched the girl move objects without any physical force. One of the scientific tests the men devised was having her stand on scales while lifting a two-thousand-pound man sitting in a chair. Inexplicably, the scales registered only a forty-pound increase in weight. She was examined by a doctor in the audience following a performance in which she caused a chair to whirl about the stage. He was amazed to find that the girl's "hands were white and moist [and] burned like hot cakes." "The Electric Girl," as she became known, insisted that her abilities were not supernatural in origin. The only effect they had on her everyday life was her inability to hold an umbrella without having it torn from her grasp.

By 1886, the rigors of performing in major cities like New York, Atlanta, Chicago and Indianapolis had taken their toll on Lulu. Following two shows in Knoxville, Tennessee, she informed her parents that she was finished with performing. Estimates of her earnings range from $50,000 to $100,000. She enrolled in Shorter College in Rome, Georgia, but withdrew in December 1986. In 1887, Lulu married her manager, Paul Atkinson. In her autobiography, Lulu credited her astounding powers to "the judicious application of body mechanics and deflection of force." She died in 1950 and was buried beside her husband in Madison, Georgia.

The Little Georgia Magnet: Dixie Haygood

MILLEDGEVILLE

Born in 1861 in Milledgeville, Dixie Haygood appeared to be destined to lead the life of a typical southern matron after marrying at the age of seventeen. However, her life was changed completely after watching a performance by Lulu Hurst in 1885. Over the next few weeks, Haygood set about learning the seemingly magical techniques that had catapulted Hurst to stardom. One month later, Haygood premiered her own act at the Academy of Music, now the Grand Opera House, in Macon in March 1885. Performing under the name Annie Abbott, Haygood earned the nickname the "Georgia Magnet" through her uncanny ability to resist being picked up off the floor by sheer strength. She was also able to lift between four and six men at the same time and to hold a billiard cue in one hand while two or three men attempted to force it to the ground. Because Haygood weighed only one hundred pounds, a few spectators drew the conclusion that she was a witch. Others assumed that she was endowed with some sort of psychic gift. Actually, she was a magician who performed seemingly impossible feats of strength through deflection, optical illusions and sleight of hand.

Unfortunately, Haygood did not achieve the same level of success in her personal life. In 1886, her husband, Deputy Marshal C.N. Haygood, was gunned down while trying to break up a fight during a prohibition rally. In 1888, she remarried, this time to a man named T.D. Embry, who had accompanied her through Alabama and Tennessee. When they arrived in Cincinnati, he informed her that the money she had earned would be safer with him than with her. She gave him all of the money she had: sixty dollars. He left town without even saying goodbye. He then asked someone to write her a letter stating that he was dead. However, when she visited his relatives in Kentucky, she learned that he was living in Mississippi. A few weeks later, the couple was divorced.

Following the breakup of her marriage, Haygood's career really took off. She was booked at venues all over the world, thrilling audiences wherever she performed. When she returned to Macon in 1894, she was a celebrity, widely considered to be one of the world's great performers. Among her admirers were Kaiser Wilhelm II of the German Empire, Emperor Franz Josef I of Austria-Hungary and Tsar Alexander III of the Russian Empire.

However, not everyone who attended her performances was impressed. Nellie Bly, a newspaper reporter, told fellow reporters that Haygood was able to resist being lifted by using the man's force against himself. During a performance, Bly asked Haygood to reveal her feet during her act. Haygood blamed her inability to perform on being out of condition. To make matters worse, the jewels and other expensive gifts she had received from world leaders made her a target for thieves. In New York in 1909, robbers stole a satchel containing $30,000 worth of jewels.

In 1912, the *Macon Telegraph* reported that Haygood believed her strength was dwindling as she aged. She died on November 21, 1915, and was buried in Memory Hill Cemetery in Milledgeville. Her grave is now a popular stopping-off point on the city's Haunted Cemetery Tour.

THE ORACLE OF THE AGES: MAYHAYLEY LANCASTER

MERIWETHER COUNTY

On October 18, 1875, Mayhayley Lancaster, Georgia's most famous clairvoyant, was born in a cabin that had been in her family for more than one hundred years. Many believed that was imbued with psychic abilities after having born with a caul, or placental sac, covering her face. She began telling fortunes at the age of twelve, although her parents made her do it outside the cabin. As a young adult, Mayhayley wore gold earrings, fancy hats, silk dresses and gold-rimmed spectacles, which enabled her to see out of her single good eye. The other one was replaced with a glass eye. Her skills as a fortuneteller attracted customers from the entire area. Mayhayley developed an uncanny ability to help locate lost rings or stolen property by falling into a trance or watching the flames in her fireplace. She was also able to determine the gender of unborn children. She soon invested her earnings as a fortuneteller into the purchase of livestock, rental property and a number of businesses. She taught at Red Oak School in Heard County in 1897. In 1908, she wrote a weekly news column for the *Franklin News and Banner*. Mayhayley claimed to have passed the bar exam, but she firmly believed that "seeing the future is my art." Nevertheless, she waged two unsuccessful campaigns for the state senate, once in 1922 and again in 1926, becoming the first woman in Georgia to run for political office.

Mayhayley Lancaster achieved national recognition in 1948. According to the book *Weird Georgia* by Jim Miles, Meriwether County was controlled at this time by a wealthy landowner named John Wallace, who had made much of his money through agriculture and the distilling and sale of bootleg whiskey. One day, Wallace discovered that Wilson Turner, one of his tenant farmers, was doing extra bootlegging without Wallace's permission. In a fit of anger, Wallace fired Turner, who decided to get even by stealing two of Wallace's cows. The sheriff arrested Turner but was forced to release him because of the lack of evidence. After his release, Turner saw Wallace and two other men waiting in a car on the courthouse square in Greenville. Turner tried to make a getaway in his truck, but it ran out of gas at the Sunset Tourist Camp just across the Coweta County line. Witnesses saw Turner's body go limp as Wallace struck him in the head with a sawed-off shotgun. Wallace tried to dispose of the corpse by dumping it down a well on his property.

Mayhayley Lancaster and John Wallace had a long-standing relationship for many years. A firm believer in her powers, Wallace had visited her once every six months, asking for help locating lost and stolen items, such as a ring, a dog and a saddle. One week after Turner's murder, Wallace visited Mayhayley Lancaster twice, once to help him find the two cows that Turner had stolen and a second time to ask her the location of the well where he had dumped the body, as it was overgrown with vegetation. When he entered Mayhayley's cabin, which she had bought after her father died, she was living with her elderly sister, Sallie. Mayhayley was wearing a long woolen skirt, high-buttoned shoes and her brother's World War I army cap. Thirty-seven dogs guarded her cabin. Once Wallace paid her—one dollar for her and a dime for her dogs—she gazed into the flames of her fire and talked to him about where the cows could be found. On his second visit to the cabin, she exclaimed, "You killed him, didn't you?" She went on to say that the well would be located and that "a brave man, a man who is true," would arrest him.

Convinced that "the witch" had told him the truth, Wallace attempted to find the well with the help of two of his tenant farmers. After the men found it, they removed the body and transported it to a moonshine pit, where they soaked it in gasoline and set it afire under two cords of wood. The next morning, the men scraped the bottom of the pit and dumped the ashes into a creek.

The task of finding Turner's body was given to state patrol sergeant J.C. Otwell and Georgia Bureau of Investigation agent Jim Hillin. They consulted Coweta County sheriff Lamar Potts, who recommended talking to Mayhayley Lancaster. She introduced herself as the "Oracle of the Age" and then told them that Wallace had visited her twice and that on his second visit, he had asked her how to find a lost body. She then sat in her chair and slipped into a trance. Suddenly, she raised her head and said, "Gone from its hiding place…men, horses, a truck, fire." With the clues that Mayhayley had given him, Potts instigated an extensive search for Turner's body. Before long, they found the well and the place where the body had been incinerated, along with a few bone fragments. Bits of brain tissue were found around the well. Investigators concluded that they had collected enough evidence to bring Wallace to trial.

Mayhayley was the last witness to be called on the first day of the trial, so she spent most of the day telling fortunes in the courthouse square. Wearing a shiny red dress decorated with snorting yellow dragons, she spoke about Wallace's two visits to her cabin. She also discussed seeing the body in a well during one of her visions, as well as Wallace's attempt to move the body. When Wallace's lawyer tried to discredit Mayhayley's psychic gifts, she sidestepped the questions. After she left the stand, Wallace was overcome with the sickening feeling that her testimony was damning. The jury found Wallace guilty. As Mayhayley had predicted, he was executed in the electric chair on November 3, 1950. She refused to attend Wallace's funeral because "he'll surely not come to mine."

Mayhayley Lancaster passed away on May 22, 1955. Even though she has been dead for many years, people still adorn her gravesite at Caney Head Methodist Church with gifts, pebbles and flowers. The fact that some people place coins on her headstone suggests that they still have faith in her power to grant their wishes.

MYSTERIES FROM THE SKIES

ODDITIES FROM ABOVE

GEORGIA

Born in Albany, New York, Charles Hoy Fort aspired to become a naturalist, amassing a large collection of seashells and minerals as a child. At age eighteen, after returning from a trip through the United States, Scotland, England and South Africa, he married his childhood sweetheart, Anna Filing. His meager earnings as a writer of newspapers and magazines barely supported them. He and Anna lived in London from 1924 to 1926 so that he could peruse the city's libraries and the British Museum. After returning to New York in 1926, he continued his search in libraries, scientific journals, magazines and newspapers for stories about strange phenomena. He compiled the thousands of notes that he took into four books, the most famous of which is *The Book of the Damned* (1919). Following his death from leukemia in 1932, the term "Fortean" was applied not only to his followers but also to unexplainable events, such as strange disappearances, levitation and spontaneous combustion. Among the most bizarre of the weird phenomena in his book are the "falls" from the sky, such as frogs, fish and flakes of meat. Over the years, a number of strange things have fallen from the skies over Georgia.

In his book *Weird Georgia*, author Jim Miles wrote about silk-like strands that fell from the sky over Savannah on October 27, 1959. Thousands of pieces of "angel hair," as it became known, were hanging from trees, telephone lines and television antennas. After a few hours, the angel hair was reported blanketing roofs and trees over Wilkes and Taliaferro Counties. Theories regarding the origin of the strange substance ranged from cobwebs to some sort of chemical material. People curious enough to pick it up discovered that it disappeared when they touched it and that it left their hands feeling sticky. Scientists determined that a species of spiders called ballooning spiders use the angel hair as a sort of parachute that enables them to float away on the wind.

Ice falling from the sky is a regular occurrence in the colder parts of the United States. In the South, snow, even in barely measurable amounts, is quite an event, especially for people who have never been up north. The residents of Georgia have had personal experience with snow, hail and sleet, usually in small amounts. However, on at least two occasions, the ice that fell from the sky was unique.

On January 31, 2017, several members of the Whitaker family were inside their home in Grayson at 7:45 a.m. when suddenly, a large chunk of ice crashed through the roof, leaving a big hole. "You can see there was a lot of debris that exploded and went everywhere," Jamey Whitaker said. His wife, Cora, was grateful that the ice had not hit the other side of the house where her daughters' rooms were located. Whitaker examined the scattered chunks of ice on the floor and concluded that it was connected to the planes that make regular flights over the house. According to a representative of the Federal Aviation Administration, the Whitakers' house could have been struck by "blue ice," which forms when liquid leaks from a commercial aircraft's lavatory system in low temperatures, causing it to freeze to the plane.

In early January 2021, a different type of ice fell across North Georgia. The spotty white showers that passed through this part of the state left behind mushy white snow pellets called graupel. Some of the residents of Carol, Haralson, Douglas, Paulding, Cobb and Gwinnett Counties claimed that these small ice formations resembled crystal rocks or Dippin' Dots. According to meteorologists, graupel starts out as a snowflake. As it floats down from the sky, it comes into contact with super-cooled water droplets that freeze to it, transforming the snowflake into a tiny ball of ice. Graupel differs from hail in that hail is harder and it makes more noise when it hits the ground.

GEORGIA'S PROJECT BLUE BOOK SIGHTINGS

GEORGIA

Project Blue Book was a compilation of UFO sightings in the United States from 1949 to 1969. All of the reports were analyzed and filed. None of the 12,618 UFO reports were found to contain evidence proving that extraterrestrial vehicles had visited the earth. A number of these sightings took place in Georgia.

On July 7, 1940, a woman told an air force agent that she saw a bright object in the shape of an electric light hanging in the sky at a forty-five-degree angle. Twelve days later, another UFO sighting appeared in the *Valdosta Daily Times*. An engraver named Ed Hopkins reported seeing a reddish-orange ball of fire that traveled through the night sky much faster than Nazi Germany's V-2 rockets. A second eyewitness who identified himself as "Hugh" said that he had seen a "fiery object" the same night.

UFO sightings continued well into the 1950s. In an Air Intelligence Report from August 5, 1952, a member of the Moody Air Force Base Band claimed to have seen three objects flying at different altitudes. On November 30, 1954, the skies over East Alabama and West Georgia were filled with aerial explosions for two hours. At first, many witnesses believed that one or more planes had crashed in the area. Around the same time, the Birmingham, Alabama control tower reported a silver object falling from the sky. Eventually, the object was identified as a meteor that had broken into fragments as it entered the atmosphere.

Two particularly memorable sightings were recorded in Turnerville in the 1960s. On June 29, 1964, Jimmy Ivester, his parents and his brothers and sisters were sitting in the living room when static interference interrupted the television program they were watching. Puzzled by what had just happened, they went out to the front porch and talked for a while. All at once, a large object appeared just above the trees. It flew close to the house before moving out toward the highway, where it hovered for a while. In the short time that the craft was visible, the onlookers noticed that it was bowl-shaped with three blinking red lights. As soon as the lights dimmed, the object rose in the air. A bright green light on the bottom of the UFO lit up the sky. The Iverson family also detected a foul smell. By the time Sheriff A.J. Chapman appeared on the scene, the UFO had returned. The sheriff saw it soaring overhead. He also caught a whiff of an awful smell. Another witness, Beauford E. Parham, saw a bright light as he was driving home that night. He claimed to

On June 29, 1964, a bowl-shaped UFO, similar to the one in the illustration, flew close to the Iverson family's house in Turnerville. *Wikimedia Commons.*

have seen a spinning object shaped like a top. It was six feet tall and eight feet wide. He was close enough to the spacecraft to see several small portholes on the bottom. After vanishing for a few seconds, it reappeared five feet in front of him. For a mile, the object kept pace with Parham's car. Suddenly, it flew over him, filling his car with a terrible smell. Afterward, Parham had a burning, tingling feeling in his arm.

The last unsolved Blue Book sighting in Georgia occurred on November 28, 1968. Conway Jones, a bank accountant from Albany, was driving through a desolate area ten miles west of Newton. Rounding a curve, he saw a bright yellowish-white light floating seventy feet over the road two hundred feet ahead of him. Later, he described that nontransparent object as being between forty and fifty feet wide. As he neared the object, a six-foot-wide ray of green light shone down, causing the radio to turn off and the engine to die. Four minutes later, the object emitted a reddish-orange glow and flew straight up in the air, completely vanishing in about fifteen seconds. Later, a representative of Moody Air Force Base stated that Jones was one of several people who had seen the UFO that night.

PRESIDENT JIMMY CARTER'S UFO SIGHTING

LEARY

Former president Jimmy Carter's highly publicized UFO sighting occurred in Leary, Georgia, in 1969. *Wikimedia Commons.*

In 1969, Jimmy Carter was visiting the Lions Club in Leary, Georgia, when he and ten other people witnessed an astounding aerial display. Carter and the others were standing outside a high school lunchroom at 7:30 p.m. when they beheld a self-luminous green light in the western sky. "It got brighter and brighter," Carter said, "and then it disappeared. It didn't have any solid substance to it. It was just a very peculiar-looking light. None of us could understand what it was."

On September 18, 1973, Governor Carter reported his sighting to an unofficial group of aerial phenomena experts. Skeptics believed that Carter had actually seen the planet Venus, which was visible in the western sky at that time. Carter, an amateur astrologer, disagreed, stating that he had seen Venus before, and what he saw was entirely different. He added that he had not seen an alien spaceship.

Following his sighting, Carter vowed never to mock anyone who claimed to have seen a UFO. In fact, when he ran for president in 1976, he said that when he was elected president, he would urge all federal agencies to make public all classified information concerning UFOs. However, after he became president, Carter retracted his previous statement in the belief that declassifying this information would threaten national security.

MYSTERIOUS DISAPPEARANCES

Benjaman Kyle: A Man in Search of Himself

RICHMOND HILL

On August 31, 2004, a Burger King cleaning lady was taking trash to a dumpster in back of the restaurant, just as she had done countless times before. On this particular day, she happened to look behind the dumpster. Lying on the ground was a naked, sunburned man. She told a police dispatcher that she thought he was dead. The paramedics took the man to St. Joseph's Hospital. Because the man had no identification, he was referred to as a "vagrant" in the police report and as "Burger King Doe" in the hospital admission form. He was found to have a rash, several red ant bites and three depressions in his skull. The doctors surmised that he was the victim of blunt force trauma. His neck and left arm were scarred as well. His scraggly beard and dirty fingernails suggested that the man had been homeless for quite a while. He could barely see because of cataracts. He appeared to be around fifty years old.

Burger King Doe's behavior indicated that he had undergone some sort of psychological trauma as well. A doctor was examining his chest when suddenly, the man began kicking and waving his arms. When a nurse asked him what his name was, he replied, "They call me B.K. around here." He also told the nurse that he had been living in the woods for seventeen years and that he thought he was from Indianapolis. He believed that he had three brothers, but he could not remember any of their names. When he was transferred to Lewis Primary Health Care Center four months later, he informed the doctors that he could recall current events, such as the election of George W. Bush as president, but he could not recall any personal information. The nurses enjoyed quizzing him about his past and adding to his growing store of self-knowledge. After a while, he could remember his first name—Benjaman, spelled with two *as*—but he did not know his last name. Benjaman thought that he had fled to Richmond from Hurricane Charley in late August 2004. Later, he recalled that his last name was Kyle.

Benjaman soon became a favorite of the nurses. He enjoyed mopping floors and making beds. Nine months after he was found, money raised through charitable donations enabled him to have his cataracts removed. When he gazed into the mirror, he told the nurses that he appeared to be twenty years older than he thought he was. Nine months after his corrective eye surgery, he began to be shuttled between hospitals and the Grace House men's shelter for several years.

Two years after arriving at the shelter, Kyle met a middle-aged nurse named Katherine Slater who took it upon herself to help him discover his true identity. She thought this goal could be achieved in only six months, but the road to self-awareness turned out to be much longer than she thought it would be. Slater contacted the FBI, which was reluctant to assist her at first because not knowing who you are is not a crime. However, Special Agent Bill Kirkconell offered to feed Kyle's fingerprints into the FBI fingerprint database and to post his photograph on its missing persons page. He also sent copies of the photos to Interpol and Canadian investigative agencies. He even checked with the U.S. Marshal Service to see if Kyle was enrolled in the witness protection program. His search was unsuccessful.

In October 2008, Kyle was interviewed on the *Dr. Phil* television show. During the interview, Kyle revealed that he thought he was born on August 29, 1948, and that he had three brothers living in Indianapolis and Denver. He ended the episode by stating that when he gazed into the mirror following his corrective eye surgery, he appeared to be much older than he thought he was.

Slater and Kyle flew back to Georgia after the taping. Kyle moved in with Slater, but because of his tendency to hoard things like catalogues and old tools, she asked him to leave in February 2011. Before he left, she bought him a cellphone and found a shelter for him in Savannah. He immediately began walking toward Florida. Once he was in Jacksonville, he contacted

John Wkstrom, a twenty-one-year-old film student from Florida State University who had expressed interest in filming a documentary about him. The film was completed in March 2011 and was submitted to be shown at the Tribeca Film Festival and the American Pavilion at the Cannes Film Festival. Kyle's story was also covered by the *Orlando Sentinel*, ABC News and New York's *Daily News*. The widespread publicity regarding Kyle's case attracted the attention of Florida senator Mike Weinstein, who helped Kyle receive a legacy identification card. Before long, Kyle was able to find work and housing.

In 2015, CeCe Moore established Kyle's identity using DNA. Moore revealed that Kyle was actually William Burgess Powell. He had left his family and car and trailer where he had been living. His family had filed a missing person's report on him. The police tracked him down to Boulder, Colorado, where he was working as a cook. Earning records filed with the Social Security Administration indicated that he had worked at several restaurants in Denver beginning in 1978. No record of his existence turned up again until Kyle was found living behind the dumpster in 2004. The intervening decades are still a blank.

THE DISAPPEARANCE OF JUSTIN GAINES

DULUTH

On November 2, 2007, an eighteen-year-old Gainesville State College freshman named Justin Gaines was one of three thousand customers taking advantage of Thirsty Thursday at Wild Bill's in Duluth. Witnesses recalled that Gaines was wearing a diamond stud earring and that he was "flashing a lot of cash." After leaving the nightclub at 2.30 a.m., Gaines called several people to see if they could pick him up. Surveillance camera footage shows him talking to an assortment of different people. He did not seem to be arguing with anybody. Another surveillance camera captured footage of Gaines making phone calls in the lobby. Gaines's whereabouts following his exit from Wild Bill's are still a mystery.

Dozens of people who were at Wild Bill's that night were interviewed by police. One theory that was developed by the Gwinnett County Sheriff's Office following the interviews was that Justin entered a car driven by a blond woman wearing a black dress. Then she and her accomplices drove him to a house in Snellville. After choking and beating Gaines, they shot him and took his money and diamond earring. At first, they threw his body in Lake Lanier from a houseboat, but after it floated to the surface a few days later, they transported it to another county, where they dumped it in a well.

One of the hundreds of people interviewed by the police department provided additional information regarding Gaines's fate. Prison inmate Dylan Glass admitted to police that he had assaulted Gaines and taken his diamond earring, but he insisted that he did not kill the college student.

Glass's mother, Thelma Ballew, not only backed up her son's story, but she also told police that she, fifty-seven-year-old Martin Leonard Willkie and another man had dumped Gaines's body in an old well in the High Shoals area. Police followed up on Ballew's lead, but when they were unable to find any trace of the missing college student, they charged her with making false statements to law officials. On September 2, police arrested Martin Leonard Willkie. They alleged that he and Dylan Glass had shot Justin Gaines. Then they and an unidentified third man placed the body in a metal toolbox and concealed it somewhere.

The search for Justin Gaines's body continued for years following his disappearance. In 2015, the remains of a man between twenty-five and forty years old were found in a wooded area in Burford. The medical examiner determined that the remains were not those of Justin Gaines. In the fall of 2019, human remains found near Lake Lanier fueled hopes that Justin Gaines's body had finally been found. However, making a DNA match with Justin Gaines has proven to be difficult. To date, there is no physical evidence supporting Glass's story or any of the theories about Gaines's disappearance.

JOHN "DAX" DUNN'S LONG FISHING TRIP

NEWMAN

In February 2020, John "Dax" Dunn, a forty-year-old mechanic, was living in Newman, Georgia, with his wife and four children. On February 14, 2020, he left Newman for a four-day fishing trip somewhere near Tampa. On February 15, he made a bank transaction in Inglis, Florida. Dunn was last seen on February 15 at a Circle K gas station in Inglis. His credit card receipt revealed that he bought Little Caesar's Pizza, two energy drinks, three packs of cigarettes and a Gatorade.

Dunn's white Nissan pickup truck was found on a private road in a slightly wooded area near the boat ramp on County Road 40. In the truck bed were fishing rods and reels. However, Dunn's keys, pistol, spear gun and life vest were not in the truck. Detectives searching the area learned that Dunn had rented a 10.5-foot green kayak and a life vest from Paddles Outdoor Rentals on February 17. The kayak was never returned to the rental agency. The Levy County Sheriff's Office, along with the Marion County Sheriff's Office, the Citrus County Sheriff's Office and the Florida Fish and Wildlife Conservation Commission, conducted an extensive search for Dunn using helicopters, boats and airplanes. Deputies also investigated fishing camps in the Crystal River and Yankeetown area. No trace of the retired U.S. Marine was ever found. At the time of this writing, Dunn is still considered a missing person.

MYSTERIOUS MONSTERS

Altamaha-ha: Georgia's Sea Serpent

DARIEN AND BUTLER ISLAND

The Altamaha River in southern Georgia is a 137-mile waterway formed by the convergence of the Oconee and Ocmulgee Rivers east of Lumber City. The river is known for its hunting, fishing, kayaking and scenic beauty. The Altamaha River is also known for its legendary sea monster, Altamaha-ha.

For centuries, the Tama Indians told stories about a huge snakelike creature with gray-green skin that lived in the river. The first published sighting of Altamaha-ha, or "Altie" for short, was reported on April 18, 1830, by a Captain Delano aboard the schooner *Eagle*. He was sailing in St. Simons Sound when a seventy-foot-long creature emerged from the watery depths. In a newspaper account of the incident, the captain described the monster as having a long neck and an alligator-shaped head. At the same time, several planters and farmers also saw the creature floating down the river. The captain dismissed the possibility that he and his men had actually seen a dolphin because they had seen scores of them before, and this animal was unlike anything they had ever seen.

People continued to report seeing a strange aquatic creature around the mouth of the Altamaha River throughout the eighteenth and nineteenth centuries. It was sighted by loggers in the 1920s, by hunters in the 1930s, by

The Altamaha River is believed to be the home of a sea serpent, the sightings of which date back to the time of the Tama Indians. *Wikimedia Commons.*

a group of Boy Scouts in the 1940s and by a couple of prison officials in the 1950s. Most of the sightings in the 1960s, 1970s and 1980s were by crabbers and fishermen. An amateur photographer took a video of an unidentified creature swimming in the river in 2010.

Of course, not all of the sightings of Altamaha-ha have been universally accepted as genuine. Many people believe that large alligator gars have been misidentified as the legendary monster. Skepticism regarding the beast's existence increased following the discovery of the decomposing remains of a strange creature in the Wolf Island National Wildlife Refuge. It turned out to be made out of a stuffed shark and papier-mâché by performance artist Zardulu. Does the fact that the original settlers came from Inverness, Scotland, the home of the Loch Ness monster, suggest that they and their descendants are inclined to see aquatic monsters?

GEORGIA'S BIGFOOT SIGHTINGS

NORTHERN GEORGIA

Sightings of the elusive creature known as Bigfoot have been reported in Georgia for many years. According to Jim Miles's book *Weird Georgia*, the earliest sighting was reported in the *Milledgeville Statesman* in June 1829. Lured by an Indian legend of a colony of "mortals of super-human dimensions" on an isolated island in Okefenokee Swamp, two men and a boy trudged for two weeks through the muck before finding a footprint eighteen inches long. The group returned home and told their friends and relatives about the "Man Mountain" that must have made the track. Eight hunters who heard the story found a trail of abnormally large footprints and followed it for several days. One evening, they were camped on a ridge when, suddenly, two of the men began firing their rifle at a huge, man-like beast that was rapidly approaching them. Hearing the screams of the monster, the other men fired their weapons as well. Undeterred by the barrage of bullets, the Bigfoot attacked the men, killing four of them before it died. Fearing retaliation by more of these creatures, the four survivors measured the beast—it was thirteen feet long—and fled the scene.

Bigfoot sightings in Georgia have continued well into the modern era. In 1951 near Valdosta, a woman was awakened by the baying of her dogs in the front yard. She and her husband walked outside and were surprised to find a large, hairy humanoid creature standing on the porch. Her husband shot at the beast, and it ran off. Not long thereafter, the woman's stepfather was sitting in his cabin one evening when he saw a hairy face staring through the window. He walked outside and fired his pistol at the creature, scaring it off into the woods. In 1997, a large humanoid-like track was discovered on Elkins Creek in Pike County. The plaster cast of the track bears little resemblance to casts of gorilla and black bear tracks.

Sightings by police officers seem to have more credibility than those by ordinary citizens. A case in point occurred in 2009 at Minnehaha Falls. Late one evening, an off-duty policeman was eating a sandwich when he saw a large man-like figure standing by the falls. His curiosity piqued, the officer walked in the figure's direction and immediately detected a pungent odor that became stronger the closer he got. He estimated that the creature stood nine to ten feet tall. The officer pulled his gun and yelled, causing the creature to run toward the right of the waterfall and up the ridge.

In 2016, Bigfoot researcher David Bakara and his wife, Melinda, opened Expedition Bigfoot, the Sasquatch Museum, in Cherry Log, Georgia. The museum includes a number of displays, such as the types of food preferred by the beasts, videotaped eyewitness accounts and plaster casts of Bigfoot footprints. In 2019, the museum posted a story on its Facebook page about a driver's encounter with a seven- to eight-foot-tall bipedal creature with a pointed head at 8:20 p.m. on May 22. He said it was walking along the side

The presence of the Bigfoot Travel Center reflects the Bigfoot activity that has been reported in Valdosta. *Wikimedia Commons.*

of the road near a small wooded area and that it had very long arms that stuck out while it walked. The driver skidded to a stop as the creature slipped into the woods. The same man had another encounter eight days later while on his way to work early in the morning in Rabun County near Layton. He said that a blackish-gray creature loped through a field to a trout stream. Exiting his truck for a better look, the man locked eyes with the beast, which by this time was only fifty feet away. The startled creature slowly faded back into the forest.

Even though crowds of people come to the museum every year, Bakara believes that many people conceal their interest in the creature. In fact, he estimates that only one out of ten people ever report their Bigfoot sightings. While no definite proof of the creature's existence has surfaced, the large number of sightings in states like Georgia cannot be easily dismissed as the product of overactive imaginations.

The Talbot County Werewolf

TALBOT COUNTY

In the mid-nineteenth century, the Burt family was one of the richest in Talbot County. Their three-hundred-acre estate was located in Pleasant Hill, not far from the tiny town of Talbotton. After Mr. Burt died at the age of thirty-seven, his wife sent their only daughter, Emily Isabella Burt, to boarding school in Paris, France. When she returned to Talbotton a few years later, people began noticing that she had changed in several small but noticeable ways. She seemed distant somehow, staring into space for no apparent reason. Some people said that she had begun sleepwalking at night. In 1840, not long after she returned, a large number of sheep and other animals were found horribly mutilated in the area. One night, an armed posse roamed the county, searching for whatever was killing their livestock. One local farmer who had lost a number of sheep offered $200 to anyone who shot the creature responsible for the rash of killings.

Most people blamed a wolf for the deaths of their livestock until an elderly farmer from Bohemia told his neighbors that werewolves tend to kill for pleasure, as this particular creature seemed to have done. He recommended melting down silver into the shape of bullets because back home in eastern Europe, people found that werewolves could be killed with silver. Armed with silver bullets, a posse was formed to track down the creature. One of the men spotted the werewolf and fired, wounding it. On close inspection, he discovered that his bullet had severed the left front paw of the beast. The next day, Emily's mother was surprised to find that her daughter had been shot in the arm. After the local doctor bandaged the wound, Mrs. Burt sent her back to Europe for treatment. Rumors soon spread throughout town that Emily's hand and wrist had been shot off. People also said that Emily was probably bitten by a werewolf the first time she had visited France. They suspected that she was being treated for lycanthropy on her second visit to France.

Their suspicions that Emily had contracted lycanthropy seemed to be confirmed when she returned from Europe, totally cured. The animal attacks on the sheep ceased as well. She inherited her father's estate following the death of her mother and spent the rest of her time in Talbotton as a respected member of the community.

NATIVE AMERICAN LEGENDS

THE CREEK DEVIL DOG

JACKSON COUNTY

Hundreds of years ago, the Creek Indians referred to the marshland east of Atlanta as Nodoroc, the "Gateway to Hell." In the middle of the swamp was said to be a huge volcano of mud. It was actually a boggy pond near the present day town of Windor. According to Creek legend, criminals were executed in this place, and their corpses were tossed into the bog, where they would be eaten by a demonic creature called the "Wog." In his book *The Early History of Jackson County, Georgia* (1914), author G.J.N Wilson describes the beast as "a jet black, long haired animal about the size of a small horse, but his legs were much shorter, the front ones being some twelve inches longer than the hind ones. This gave him something of the appearance of a huge dog sitting on its tail." It had a bear-like head and great white teeth protruding from under its lips. Its most distinctive characteristic was its tail, which was uniformly thick and ending in a cluster of white hair. White wrote that the tail "was in constant motion from side to side, not as a dog wags his tail, but with a quick upward curve which brought it down with a whizzing sound that could be distinctly heard at least when twenty-five or thirty steps distant."

According to one Creek legend, the beautiful daughter of the chief of the Creeks, Umausauga, rejected the advances of a suitor from the Choctaw tribe. Outraged by the girl's refusal, the warrior killed her and ran into the woods. Before long, he was apprehended by the girl's father and brother, who removed his heart and threw it to the wolves. They then dragged his corpse to Nodoroc and gave it to the Wog. The Choctaws dispatched several war parties to take vengeance on the Creek, but every one of them was eaten by the demonic dog.

In another Creek legend, a woman named Fenceruga killed and ate one of her children. Chief Urocasca ordered a band of warriors to take her to Nodoroc and toss her headfirst into the boiling pond. The resounding splash made by her body awakened the sleeping Wog, which rolled over and over again in the mud and thrashed its tail. The screaming ghost of the mother is said to be chased by a crowd of vengeful children for eternity.

FANNIN COUNTY FAIRY CROSSES

BLUE RIDGE AND MINERAL BLUFF

Staurolite is highly prized by rock collectors because of its unique shape. The name is a combination of two Greek words: *stauros*, meaning "cross," and *lithos*, meaning "stone." Formed under great pressure between sixty and five hundred million years ago, staurolite is composed of iron, silica and aluminum. The cross shape is created when the rock's composite minerals crystalize in twin form.

In an article titled "Fairy Crosses Found in Fannin County," author Christy Reece recounts two legends associated with the creation of the fairy crosses. One of the tales dates back to the forced removal of sixty thousand Native Americans by the United States government between 1830 and 1850. Some people say that the fairy crosses were formed from the tears of Native Americans on the Trail of Tears. An even older story deals with the Yunwi Tsunsdi, or Little People. They were dancing in their

Fairy crosses found in Fanning County are said to be formed from the tears of the Yunwi Tsunsdi, also known as the Little People. *Wikimedia Commons.*

secret gathering place when they learned of the death of their creator on the cross. The tears of the heartbroken Little People crystalized when they struck the ground, forming the fairy crosses.

Thousands of rock hounds have combed Fannin County for the fairy crosses, not just because of their appearance but also because of their supernatural qualities. Supposedly, they bring good luck to anyone who finds them. They are also said to have the power to protect people from accidents and illness. A number of famous people have been known to carry them. Legend has it that Pocahontas gave John Smith a fairy cross to keep him safe. Thomas Edison and Woodrow Wilson owned fairy crosses. Theodore Roosevelt even had an amulet fashioned from a fairy cross.

Fort Mountain

CHATSWORTH

Located in Fort Mountain State Park, Fort Mountain is part of a small mountain range called the Cohutta Mountains. The mountain's name comes from an 885-foot-long stone wall that meanders around the peak. The ancient wall, which may date as far back as AD 400 to 500, is 12 feet thick and up to 7 feet high. Around the wall are cairns, stone rings, part of a gateway and twenty-nine pits.

A number of theories have been generated to explain the origin of the wall. For many years, Hernando de Soto was thought to have built the wall in 1540 as a defense against the Creek Indians, until a researcher found that the explorer remained in the area for only two weeks, which was not nearly enough time to build the huge wall. According to Cherokee legend, the wall was erected by the "moon-eyed" people who lived in the southern Appalachian region of the United States before the Cherokee occupied the territory. Benjamin Smith Barton first made reference to the moon-eyed people in a book published in 1797. The Cherokee gave them the name "moon-eyed people" because they could see better at night than in the daytime. The Cherokee also believed that they had white skin, blue eyes and beards. They were much smaller in stature than the Cherokee people.

One early historian believed that the moon-eyed people were albinos descended from the Kuna people of Panama. However, for many years, some historians have believed that they might have been descended from a

The Cherokee believed that the "moon-eyed" people erected the 885-foot-long stone wall on top of Fort Mountain. *Wikimedia Commons.*

Welsh prince named Madoc a Gwynedd. The story goes that after his father died, he and one of his brothers, Rhirid, gathered up a few followers in 1170 and sailed toward North America. They are said to have landed around Mobile Bay, Alabama. After a time, Prince Madoc went back to Wales and returned with ten ships. His mission was to make a permanent home for themselves in the New World. Some people think that Prince Madoc and his band built the wall on Fort Mountain and similar stone fortifications near De Soto Falls in Alabama and in Chattanooga, Tennessee. In 1783, a Cherokee chief named Oconostota told Tennessee governor John Sevier that the mounds in the state were built by white men whom the Cherokee had driven out of the area. Despite the research conducted by hundreds of explorers, geologists, historians and archaeologists, the legend of the moon-eyed people remains just that—a legend.

The Nacoochee Indian Mound

HELEN

Between 1350 and 1600, what is now known as the Hardman Farms was a traditional burial ground for the Chickasaw. In the late 1870s, Captain

James H. Nichols bought a plot of pasture and farmland in Helen, Georgia. Sitting in the middle of the pasture was an Indian mound. Unaware of the archaeological value of the site, Nichols cut two feet off the top of the mound and erected a gazebo. In 1893, Calvin Hunnicutt purchased the property. The next owner was Larmartine Griffin Hardman, who bought the property in 1903. Later on, Hardman's family donated the Hardman Farms to the State of Georgia. In 1915, a team from the Smithsonian Institute excavated the mound. They discovered seventy-five burials and artifacts dating back to the south Appalachian Mississippi culture.

The legend of the Nacoochee Indian Mound focuses on Sautee, a Chickasaw warrior, and Nacoochee, the Cherokee princess. After accidentally meeting each other while walking separately through the woods, the couple immediately fell in love. When Nacoochee's father learned of the love affair, he ordered Sautee to be tossed from the top of Yonah Mountain. Unwilling to continue living without Sautee, Nacoochee jumped from the top of the mountain to her death below. In a variant of the legend, Nacoochee jumped

According to Chickasaw legend, two star-crossed lovers, Nacoochee and Sautee, are buried in the mound that bears her name. *Wikimedia Commons.*

in front of Sautee just before he was about to be shot by a Cherokee arrow. The arrow passed through Nacoochee and pinned her to Sautee. Both lovers tumbled off the mountain to its base below. According to most versions of the legend, they were buried in the mound that bears Nacoochee's name. However, some say that they were buried in a mound located where Sautee Creek and the Chattahoochee converge. After an archaeological team from the University of Georgia excavated the area in 2004 and found no evidence that the Cherokee had lived there during this time, they concluded there is probably more myth than fact in the legend of Nacoochee and Sautee.

STONE PILE GAP

DAHLONEGA

At the intersection of State Road 60 and U.S. 19, drivers headed ten miles north of Dahlonega encounter a large pile of stones. According to a legend passed down by the Cherokee tribe for centuries, a Cherokee princess asked the witch of Cedar Mountain for a spell that would keep her young and beautiful forever. The witch informed her that if she drank from the medicinal spring, the Great Spirit would grant her wish. Anxious to keep her youthful appearance forever, the princess followed the witch through the woods to the magic spring. As she eagerly took her first drink, the witch told her that her beauty would be enhanced with each sip.

When the princess returned to her tribe, she was besieged with suitors. Now that she could afford to be choosy, she turned them all down. One of these men, Trahlyta, did not just walk away dejectedly like the others did. Trahlyta abducted her and held her captive. Because the princess was unable to follow the witch's instructions, her beauty slowly faded. Weeping tears of gold, the girl requested that she be buried at a mountain location where everyone would pass by. Generations of Cherokees have dropped stones on the pile in the hope that the maiden's spirit would make them happy and beautiful.

Stone Pile Gap, as the rock pile is called, seems to be protected by some sort of curse. It is said that anyone who takes a stone from the pile will suffer misfortune. During the two failed attempts by the Georgia Department of Highways to move the pile, at least two workers died. Drivers toss rocks and trinkets out of their car windows in the hope that their wishes will be

Stone Pile Gap at the intersection of State Road 60 and U.S. 19 marks the grave of a Cherokee princess who perished in her quest to remain beautiful forever. *Wikimedia Commons.*

granted. The appearance of Stone Pile Gap is believed to have changed little over the years.

According to writer Peter Eury, the witch's spring has also become the stuff of legend. Located about a mile from Stone Pile Gap, Porter Springs, as it is now known, was said to have been one of the possible candidates for the Fountain of Youth that Hernando de Soto sent his conquistadors to investigate. In the nineteenth century, the spring's reputed curative power attracted hundreds of visitors to the resort town of Porter Springs. The hotel that housed them is long gone, but the legend that drew people here in the first place remains.

TALLULAH GORGE

TALLULAH FALLS

The thousand-foot-deep crevice known as Tallulah Gorge was formed by the confluence of the Tallulah River and the Tugaloo River. The Cherokee

According to Cherokee legend, Princess Tallulah and her white lover fell to their deaths in the gorge that was named after her. *Wikimedia Commons.*

Indians believed that a race of little people called the Yunwi who lived in the gorge tricked passersby into falling into the deepest canyon in North America east of the Rocky Mountains. In a variant of the legend, the little people abducted trespassers and threw them into the river at the bottom of the gorge. The Yunwi believed that their cave on the highest side of the gorge was the entrance to the happy hunting grounds.

An Indian legend centers on a rock formation in the gorge. Tallulah, the beautiful daughter of Chief Grey Eagle, was walking on one of the trails near the gorge when she found a white hunter who had lost his way. She brought the young man into Grey Eagle's camp, where she arranged for him to spend the night. Tallulah's suitors became jealous of the attention Tallulah was lavishing on the white hunter and talked her father into sentencing him to death. That night, they bound him and took him to a rock outcropping in the gorge. Tallulah arrived on the scene just in time to see her lover thrown into the gorge. Preferring death over life without him, she leapt into the canyon.

UNIVERSITY LEGENDS

Augusta State University

AUGUSTA

The Academy of Richmond County was founded in 1785 as a high school that offered college-level courses. Degrees earned from the academy allowed students to enter college as sophomores or juniors. After 1909, the Augusta Board of Education assumed control of the academy. In 1925, as the school was being enlarged, it adopted a new identity as the Junior College of Augusta. In 1957, the Junior College became a separate entity and was moved to its present location on the site of the U.S. Army arsenal, which had closed two years earlier. The institution acquired a new name, Augusta State University, in 1996. In 2012, the board renamed the school Georgia Regents University after a merger with Georgia Health Sciences University. In 2015, the name was changed to Augusta University.

Bellevue Hall is steeped in legends. For many years, people believed that it dated back to 1806, when it served as the summer home of Freeman Walker. However, it was actually built in 1850 for a military storekeeper named John M. Galt. He and his wife had two daughters, Emily and Lucy. The story goes that Emily fell in love with one of the soldiers stationed at the arsenal. After they became engaged, she delighted in showing off her ring. After the Civil War started in 1861, Emily and Lucy scratched their names

Bellevue Hall is believed to be haunted by the ghosts of Emily and Lucy, the daughters of a military storekeeper named John Galt.

on an upstairs window with the diamond ring. A few months later, Emily's fiancé was sent to battle. When she received word that he had been killed, the heartbroken young woman jumped from an upper-story window and killed herself. However, according to author Austin Hendricks, Emily was driven mad with grief and committed to an insane asylum, where she died. Visitors to Bellevue Hall claim to have seen the apparitions of two little girls, probably Emily and Lucy, playing in the hallway. People have also heard Emily and her lover arguing about his decision to enlist in the army.

Erected in 1829, the commandant's house was one of the first buildings in the U.S. arsenal. In 1915, Colonel J. Walker Benet took up residence in the house with his son, Stephen Vincent Benet. Stephen called the old house home until 1915, when he entered Yale University. He went on to become a Pulitzer Prize–winning author, known for such works as *John Brown's Body* and "The Devil and Daniel Webster."

The Stephen Benet House is also believed to be haunted. The story goes that in the mid-1800s, an officer lived there with his wife, a vain woman who spent exorbitant amounts of money on clothes, which were among her

The ghosts of a vain woman and a young man who loved apple pie haunt the Stephen Benet House. *Wikimedia Commons.*

most prized possessions. Her indulgent husband started every morning by bringing her a cup of tea before he went hunting. One morning, the maid walked into the bedroom with the intention of making the bed and was shocked to find her lying on the floor, dead. The physician determined that she had been poisoned. Accusatory fingers were immediately pointed at her husband, who denied the charges. No one was brought to trial for the woman's murder. His wife's restless spirit has been seen staring at herself in the mirror and rattling the coat hangers in the closet.

A spirit dubbed the "Apple Pie Ghost" also haunts the Stephen Benet House. This apparition was the nephew of a commander who lived in the house during the Civil War. Because the young man was paid more than the average soldier at the arsenal, the other men harbored ill feeling toward him. Legend has it that one day, the commander's nephew walked over to the apple orchard to pick apples for pie. After he had filled his bucket, he returned home and was shot as he walked up the steps. People say that his ghost, still hungering for a piece of apple pie, is responsible for opening and closing the cabinet doors and the oven door.

Berry College

MOUNT BERRY

Founded in 1902 by Martha Berry in Floyd County, Berry College quickly became known as one of the most prominent four-year liberal arts colleges in the United States. The college's donations began to decline after Berry's death in 1942. By the time World War II ended in 1945, the school's mission was viewed by many as outdated. Over the next five years, a succession of presidents attempted to improve the school's image. Thanks to President John R. Bertrand, who elevated the quality of the college's professional programs, Berry College was accredited by the Southern Association of Colleges and Schools in 1957. Today, Berry College has a student population of around two thousand. The college has become widely known for the movies that have been filmed there, like *Sweet Home Alabama*, and its large number of ghost stories.

Berry University is unique among haunted colleges in that it has haunted roads as well as haunted buildings. Students say that people who drive along CCC Road can count seven bridges, but when they drive back up the road, they can count only six. Stretch Road is said to be haunted by the Green Lady. In the standard version of the legend, she was a student who was fighting with her boyfriend one night while they were driving on Stretch Road. She became so angry that she insisted he let her out on the road so she could walk back home. Furious, the young man waited until she had exited the car. As he backed up so that he could turn the car around, he accidentally ran over his girlfriend. In a variant of the tale, the young woman was walking back home when she accidentally fell off the bridge and drowned in the creek. In another version, the young man and woman were riding their bikes down Stretch Road one dark night. After a while, they got into an argument and rode off in different directions. After a minute or so, he turned around and rode after her, totally unaware that she had changed directions and was pursuing him. The two collided, and the girl perished a while later from a fatal head injury. Today, students driving along Stretch Road at night claim to have sighted her ghost walking along the road. Some say they have looked in the rearview mirror and seen her sitting in the back seat.

East and West Mary Residence Halls are said to be haunted by the ghost of a student who hanged herself in the tower between the buildings after finding out that her boyfriend was killed in action in World War II. Students who have entered the room in the tower where her body hung for three days

A young woman who hanged herself haunts the tower between the East and West Mary Residence Halls. *Wikimedia Commons.*

before being discovered claim to have walked into cold spots at particularly hot times of the year. They have also heard the faint sound of a woman crying and screaming in the tower.

A much smaller haunted site on campus is Roosevelt Cabin. Built in 1902 as a guest room, it served as Martha Berry's home for five years. The cabin was named after President Theodore Roosevelt, who ate lunch there in 1910. Students who have walked past the cabin late at night have seen a light shining through a window on the eve of the roof when the cabin was unoccupied.

BRENAU UNIVERSITY

GAINESVILLE

The institution now known as Brenau University started out in 1878 as the Georgia Baptist Female Seminary. In 1900, H.J. Pearce bought the seminary and renamed it, combining parts of two words: the German *brennen*, which means "to burn," and the Latin word *aurum*, which means "gold." The school's motto—"As Gold Refined by Fire"—reflects the melding of the two words. At that time, students were given the freedom to choose liberal arts courses as electives. Another radical innovation was instituted in 1860 when both male and female students were given the option of attending night and weekend courses. Brenau College changed its name to Brenau University in 1992 because of its comprehensive programs of study. Online courses were added to the curriculum in 1998. Brenau's online college was established between 2002 and 2005. Brenau University celebrated its 140th anniversary in 2018.

One of the buildings that was constructed back when the school housed the Georgia Baptist Female Seminary is Pearce Auditorium. When it was dedicated on May 21, 1897, the seven-hundred-seat opera house was hailed as the largest of its kind in the South. Like many old campus buildings, Pearce Auditorium has a haunted past. Its resident ghost is the spirit of a young woman known only as Agnes. She is said to have hanged herself from the diving board of the pool under the auditorium. Legend has it that she decided to end it all because the professor she fell in love with did not return her affections. Others believe that she killed herself because she was not accepted into a sorority. Since the early 1940s, her presence has been sensed in the residence halls and in the balcony and on the stage of Pearce Auditorium. Back then, students reported seeing a fleeting image of someone standing behind them while they were fixing their hair early in the morning. Another student at that time returned to her dorm room after class to find that all of the pennies she had been saving in a jar had been dumped out onto the floor. When she bent over to pick them up, she was shocked to find they were all heads up. In the twenty-first century, students complain that computers occasionally turn back on after they have been shut down. Many students have complained about having their lingerie misplaced or finding the doors to their rooms locked. The lights in Pearce Hall have also turned on by themselves after they were turned off, giving rise to the belief that Agnes prefers the dark. In 2013, a photograph was taken of a misty entity standing on the stage of Pearce Auditorium. Countless students have attempted to make contact with Agnes with the help of Ouija boards in Pearce Auditorium.

Agnes's identity has been a matter of speculation for over half a century. According to one theory, she was Agnes Galloway from North Carolina. However, this theory was debunked after researchers revealed that she

Students say that a girl named Agnes haunts Pearce Auditorium after she hanged herself from the diving board. *Wikimedia Commons.*

died from tuberculosis in 1929, several years after graduating from Brenau University. Some people believe that the ghost is the spirit of the wife of H.J. Pearce. Kathy Amos, retired director of the Brenau University Center for Lifetime Study, believes that the girl's spirit acquired the name Agnes after a play that was performed on the Pearce stage years ago.

Not surprisingly, the stories of the haunting of Pearce Auditorium have attracted a number of ghost-hunting groups to the university over the years. The Atlanta-based group Ghost Hounds recorded several indistinct voices on their voice recorders. In 2011, Amos and Denise Roffe, the founders of the Southeastern Institute of Paranormal Research, spent the night in the auditorium with two other ghost hunters. One of their voice recorders recorded the faint sound of someone gently weeping. In the book *Georgia Ghosts*, Brenau University student Brittany Bell told author Nancy Roberts that she was sleeping in her dorm room in East Hall one night when she heard someone softly sobbing for several minutes. The spectral crying sounds continued for several nights. Her most frightening experience happened one night when she woke up and saw the figure of a young woman hanging from a rope tied around a light fixture. Could this have been the room where Agnes hanged herself?

The large number of reports of paranormal activity on the campus of Brenau University could lead one to believe that the campus really is haunted. On the other hand, the ghost legends could have arisen as an attempt to explain the strange creaks and moans that the wood in old buildings sometimes makes. Who can really say for sure?

GEORGIA COLLEGE

MILLEDGEVILLE

The institution now known as Georgia College has its origins in the Georgia Normal and Industrial College, a two-year college that was founded in 1889. When the Main Building was completed in 1891, the Old Governor's Mansion served as a dormitory. The school became a four-year college in 1917. The college's name was changed to Georgia State College for Women in 1922. A student theatrical competition called the Golden Slipper was initiated in 1935. One of the college's most illustrious graduates, author Flannery O'Connor, enrolled in the college as a freshman in 1941. It was chosen as one of four colleges for the training of U.S. Navy WAVES in 1943. Its name was changed to the Woman's College of Georgia in 1961. A three-year renovation of the Old Governor's Mansion began in 1964, the same year the school admitted its first African American student. The school became coeducational in 1961. Four years later, its name was changed to Georgia College.

Designed by Charles Cluskey in the high Greek Revival style, Georgia's Old Governor's Mansion was built by Timothy Porter in 1839. It was the private residence of Georgia's governors until 1868. Among the important issues that were debated here were slavery and gender roles. On November 23, 1864, General William Tecumseh Sherman used the Governor's Mansion as his headquarters. The building stood empty after the seat of government was moved to Atlanta. Then in 1889, it became the founding building of the Georgia Normal and Industrial College, now known as Georgia College. A lengthy restoration process that was initiated in 2001 was completed in three years. The Old Governor's Mansion is now a historic house museum where the history of the state is told through hundreds of artifacts. History is also the basis for the ghost stories that people have been telling about the old building for years.

The delicious aroma of meals prepared by a ghostly cook named Molly permeates the halls of the Old Governor's Mansion.

The ghosts announce their presence in the mansion in a variety of ways. The museum staff can tell that the ghosts have been active during the night when they open up the museum and find that the linens have been tossed across the bedrooms. The pungent odor of cigar smoke indicates that the culprit is probably a male spirit. The ghost of a former cook named Molly might be responsible for the delicious aroma of her favorite dishes: blueberry muffins, pork and black-eyed peas. One time, when Molly apparently let potatoes on the stove burn, the staff called the fire department. Despite the acrid smell that permeated the kitchen, the firemen were unable to locate the source.

SAVANNAH COLLEGE OF ART AND DESIGN

SAVANNAH

The Savannah College of Art and Design (SCAD) was founded in 1978, with campuses in Savannah, Atlanta and Lacoste, France. One of the first buildings that the nonprofit art school restored and repurposed in Savannah was the Savannah Volunteer Guard Armory, which is now Poetter Hall. A newer building that became part of the college housed the downtown Motor Lodge in the 1960s. Located at Bull Street, the hotel offered out-of-towners a cheap place to spend the night. Just before the chain went out of business in 1993, SCAD purchased the former hotel in 1990 with the intention of converting it into a dormitory called the Oglethorpe House. According to students, some of those former guests have not checked out.

The most haunted room in the dormitory is undoubtedly room 634. The story goes that in the 1970s, a prostitute and her six-year-old son were staying in that room. One night, the woman left her son alone in the room. He was sitting on the balcony when one of the marbles he was playing with rolled off the edge. He climbed up on the railing to see where the marble had fallen and lost his balance. The child fell six stories to his death. The boy's mother was so devastated by her loss that several weeks later, she jumped off the same railing. For years, dorm residents have heard disembodied footsteps and piercing screams at night. Sleeping students have been awakened in the middle of the night by the sound of someone shouting in the room. Some students claim to have heard someone wearing high heels running down the middle of the hall. Others have heard the sound of marbles rolling in the

The ghost of a little boy haunts Oglethorpe House, a former hotel, at the Savannah College of Art and Design. *Wikimedia Commons.*

hallway. A male student had just returned from class when he noticed small wet footprints leading from the shower to the bathroom door.

The best-known ghost in the dormitory is the spirit of Gracie Watson, a little girl whose father operated the Pulaski Hotel at the corner of Bull and Bryant Streets, not far from the Oglethorpe House. She died of pneumonia in 1889. Her transparent form has been seen wandering through the rooms and hallways of the dormitory. The sounds of marbles dropping and rolling on the floor could be attributed to Gracie, who enjoyed playing in the lobby of the Pulaski Hotel.

Some of the paranormal activity in the dormitory does not seem to have a specific source. A good example is the sound of a stool scraping on the floor of room 416. A student living in an unspecified room on the student floor recalled being awakened one night by the sound of a toilet flushing on its own. One wonders if the spirits of some of the sad, lonely people who stayed at the downtown Motor Lodge years ago are trying to get the attention that is long overdue.

UNIVERSITY OF GEORGIA

ATHENS

On January 27, 1785, the University of Georgia became the first university in the United States to be granted a state charter. Abraham Baldwin is generally viewed as the founder of the university because he wrote the original charter. In 1786, Baldwin became the first president of the university. After Baldwin was elected senator, Josiah Meigs took his place as president. He was also the only professor at the time. Approximately one hundred students were enrolled in the university in 1859. However, in 1863, the university closed for the remainder of the Civil War. When the university reopened in 1866, only eighty students remained. In 1872, the Georgia State College of Agriculture and Mechanic Arts (A&M) separated from the University of Georgia. In 1903, the formerly all-male university admitted women to the State Normal School, which had been established in 1893. In 1941, the University of Georgia lost its accreditation by the Southern Association of Colleges and Schools when Governor Eugene Talmadge fired the dean of the College of Education, Walter Coking, on the charge that the dean favored racial integration. On January 6, 1961, the District Court forced the University of

Georgia to admit two Black students, Hamilton E. Holmes and Charlayne Hunter. In 2001, two new schools were added: the College of Environment and Design and the School of Public and International Affairs. By 2020, the University of Georgia had seventeen schools and colleges. It is also listed in the top five of many lists of the top ten most haunted college campuses.

The building now known as Waddell Hall is the second-oldest structure on campus. Its original name was Philosophical Hall, and it was built in 1821. In the 1950s, it was renamed Waddell Hall in honor of Moses Waddell, who was president of the university between 1819 and 1829. For many years, it was used as a dormitory and laboratory, gymnasium, boardinghouse and classroom building. In the 1970s, it housed the agricultural college. In the 1990s, it served as the Dean Rusk Center for International and Comparative Law. Waddell Hall now houses the Office of Special Events. Ironically, some of the most "special" events on campus—the ghostly type—have taken place inside Waddell Hall.

The ghost that haunts Waddell Hall is a remnant of the period when the building was used as a dormitory. In his book *Haunted Halls of Ivy*, author Daniel W. Barefoot says that after World War I ended in 1919, a young soldier who had returned home heard rumors that his girlfriend had started seeing another man while he was away. Determined to uncover the truth, he decided to have a heart-to-heart with the girl in his friend's dorm room. When she refused to resume their love affair, the soldier flew into a rage. A few minutes later, two gunshots resounded from the room. When the campus police barged into the room, they found the corpses of the young couple and a suicide note written by the soldier. For years, students and staff have heard the residual sounds of a loud, angry argument and gunshots where no one is present. Paranormal investigators have captured orbs—glowing balls of light—with their cameras.

One of the university's other nineteenth-century buildings, the Lustrat House, is also believed to be haunted. It was built in 1847 as a faculty residence. One of the first occupants of the building was Dr. Charles Morris, the chair of the English Department and a former Confederate officer. In 1903, the house was moved to its present location at 230 South Jackson Street, despite the objections of Dr. Morris. The next year, Professor Joseph Lustrat and his family moved into the house that now bears his name.

After a while, the Lustrats realized that the spirit of the late Dr. Morris had never really left. Mrs. Lustrat was the first family member to see the professor's ghost. She was in the dining room when suddenly, she saw a ghostly figure sitting at a desk near the window. Before long, her children and

Eerie knocking sounds echo through the hidden wing in Joe E. Brown Hall, where a student committed suicide over break.

her husband started seeing Dr. Morris's ghost sitting by the fireplace. Since Dr. Lustrat's death in 1927, the Lustrat House has been repurposed several times. Today, the school's Legal Affairs Department is located there. People who work there have seen Dr. Morris's ghost, dressed in his Confederate uniform or a flowered nightshirt, floating down the stairs.

One of the University of Georgia's best-known hauntings takes place at Joe E. Brown Hall, which was named after Governor Joseph E. Brown. It was built in 1932 as a men's dormitory. In 1971, during Christmas break, a male student hanged himself in his dorm room. His death was unnoticed until several weeks later, when students returning from break were drawn to his room by the pungent odor of decaying flesh. Time and time again, janitors have attempted, unsuccessfully, to remove the stains made by bodily fluids. Students living in the wing complained about the stench coming from the "suicide room." Because of the effect the room was having on the morale of dorm residents, the university sealed off the entire wing when Joe E. Brown Hall was converted into office space. In fact, the only evidence that the wing ever existed is a staircase leading to nowhere. The wing may be gone, but the ghost stories remain. Students say that when the building is empty, one can hear spectral knocking sounds coming from the hidden wing.

The Ware-Lyndon House, a Greek Revival home, was built in 1850 in Licksklitte, a trendy nineteenth-century neighborhood. When a druggist named Edward S. Lyndon purchased the house in 1880, much of the acreage had already been sold off. In 1939, the City of Athens converted the building into government offices. During World War II, it housed the local USO. For the next fifteen years, it was taken over by the Recreation Department. After the house was restored, the Lyndon House Arts Foundation was established for the maintenance of the house. In 1976, the Ware-Lyndon House was listed in the National Register of Historic Places. The ghost haunting the historic house is believed to be the spirit of Dr. Lyndon, who served as a surgeon during the Civil War. According to Kyra Posey's article in *The Red and Black*, Dr. Lyndon suffered some sort of nervous breakdown during the war, probably because of all the trauma he had witnessed. Bouts of insomnia plagued him for the rest of his life. Unwilling to practice medicine after the war, he became a druggist. Eyewitnesses describe him as a dignified-looking

Many people believe that the man dressed in black who has been seen pacing back and forth on the landing of the Ware-Lyndon House is the spirit of Dr. Edward S. Lyndon, who suffered from insomnia following his service as a surgeon in the Civil War.

The sisters of Alpha Gamma Delta believe that their house is haunted by the host of a jilted bride named Isabel.

man wearing a white shirt, tie, black pants and shoes. His ghost appears to be lost in thought, pacing back and forth on the landing.

In 1896, William Winstead Thomas built the home that has been called the Wedding Cake House as an engagement present for his daughter, Isabel, and her fiancé, Richard W. Johnson. The story goes that on the day of their wedding, her husband-to-be left Isabel standing at the altar. With tears streaming down her face, she returned home and hanged herself in her bedroom. In 1904, George Henry Hulme became the next owner of the house. Nine years later, it was bought by former senator James Yancey Carithers. Following his death, a local sorority chapter—Alpha Gamma Delta—acquired the house.

Over the years, the ghost of the jilted bride has become a very active presence in the sorority house. Many of the paranormal occurrences can best be described as poltergeist-like. Lights and faucets turn off and on by themselves. Some of the girls have heard chairs scraping across the floor of the attic. Invisible hands have been heard playing the piano. A girl who lived in the room where Isabel reportedly hanged herself complained that the closet door repeatedly opened on its own. Apparently, the ghost of Isabel Thomas does not want her, or her sad story, to be forgotten.

YOUNG HARRIS COLLEGE

YOUNG HARRIS

A circuit-riding Methodist minister named Artemas Lester founded McTyeire Institute, named after the village where the school was located. The college was supported financially by a college farm, which employed students who could not pay tuition. When McTyeire began experiencing financial difficulties, a sizable donation by Judge Young L.G. Harris proved to be enough to prevent the school from closing. Both the school and the town where it was built were renamed Young Harris Institute in 1895. Since the death of benefactor Margaret Adger Pitts in 1998, Young Harris College has received yearly proceeds and dividends. The proceeds are used primarily for religious programs, scholarships and maintenance of the campus. Young Harris College was a two-year school until 2008, when the Southern Association of Colleges and Schools granted it four-year accreditation. Today, the college offers bachelor of arts, bachelor of fine arts and bachelor of science degrees in over thirty majors.

The most haunted building on campus is undoubtedly the Clegg Building. Named after Charles Clegg, who was president of Young Harris College from 1950 to 1963, the Clegg Building was erected shortly after his death. Many students believe that the spirit of the former president is the ghost that plays the organ and walks across the stage. He is a friendly spirit who, students say, has helped them remember their lines on stage and has found props that were misplaced. In an article that appeared in the campus newspaper, *Enotah Echoes*, on October 27, 2010, staff writer Hailey Silvey interviewed longtime campus employee Dale Cochran, who said that he had a number of strange experiences while working in the shop in the Clegg Building. He heard disembodied voices call his name when no one else was around. On one occasion, he was walking toward the stage when he saw someone standing in the aisle. As he walked around the strange figure, he said, "Excuse me." When he turned back around, the figure was gone. At that moment, he realized that he had had an encounter with Charlie, as the ghost is known.

Although Charlie is not a malevolent spirit, he has inadvertently frightened people who have come upon him unexpectedly. A good example is a young woman who was listening to CDs while working in the basement. Suddenly, the pile of CDs that she had placed on a stool fell onto the floor. Unconcerned, she picked up the CDs and went back to work. The second

"Charlie," the ghost of former president Charles Clegg, haunts Clegg Hall on the campus of Young Harris College. *Wikimedia Commons.*

time the CDs fell over, the young woman grabbed them off the floor and left the building in a hurry. She never again returned to the Clegg Building by herself.

Like many students who attend haunted campuses, the students at Young Harris College are intrigued by the ghost stories. "Clegging" has become a rite of passage for many students at Young Harris College, who venture into the Clegg Building at night in the hope of hearing his ghost play the organ or piano. One of these students was Kelly Bryson from Anderson, South Carolina. "I recently went ghost hunting in Clegg and had some weird experiences," Bryson said. "I will not be going in there by myself at night again."

WORKS CITED

BOOKS

Adkins, Tracy. *Ghosts of Athens: History and Haunting of Athens, Georgia*. Scotts Valley, CA: Createspace, 2016.

Akamatsu, Rhetta. *Haunted Marietta*. Charleston, SC: The History Press, 2009.

Avena, Dianna. *Roswell: History, Haunts and Legends*. Charleston, SC: The History Press, 2007.

Barefoot, Daniel W. *Haunted Halls of Ivy*. Winston-Salem, NC: John F. Blair, Publisher, 2004.

Barnes, Margaret Anne. *Murder in Coweta County*. New York: Pelican, 1983.

Brown, Alan. *Haunted Georgia*. Mechanicsburg, PA: Stackpole Press, 2008.

Caskey, James. *Haunted Savannah: The Official Guidebook to Savannah Haunted History Tour*. Savannah, GA: Bonaventure Books, 2005.

Castel, Albert. *Kennesaw Mountain and the Atlanta Campaign*. Fort Washington, PA: Eastern National, 2015.

DeBolt, Margaret. *Savannah Spectres*. Brookfield, MO: Donning Company, 1984.

Dolgner, Beth. *Georgia Spirits and Specters*. Atglen, PA: Schiffer Publishing, 2009.

Easley, Nicole Carlson. *Savannah Folklore*. Atglen, PA: Schiffer Publishing, 2010.

Goodwin, David, and Troy Taylor. *Soldiers and the Supernatural*. Decatur, IL: Whitechapel Press, 2013.

Harding, Arthur McCracken. *Astronomy: The Splendor of the Heavens Brought Down to Earth*. New York: Garden City Publishing Company, 1940.

Harris, Michael, and Linda Sickler. *Historic Haunts of Savannah*. Charleston, SC: The History Press, 2014.

Kennedy, Frances H. *The Civil War Battlefield Guide*. Boston: Houghton Mifflin Company, 1990.

Mack, Tom. *Hidden History of Augusta*. Charleston, SC: The History Press, 2015.

Miles, Jim. *Weird Georgia*. Nashville, TN: Cumberland House Publishing, Inc., 2000.

Moore, Dot. *No Remorse: The Rise and Fall of John Wallace*. Montgomery, AL: New South Books, 2011.

———. *Oracle of the Ages*. Montgomery, AL: New South Books, 2001.

Norman, Michael, and Beth Scott. *Haunted America*. New York: Tor, 1994.

Puckett, Martha Mizzell. *Snow White Sands*. Douglas: South Georgia College, 1975.

Rhodes, Don. *Georgia Myths & Legends*. Guilford, CT: Globe Pequot, 2016.

Roberts, Nancy. *Georgia Ghosts*. Winston-Salem, NC: John F. Blair, Publisher, 1997.

Rousseau, David. *Savannah Ghosts*. Atglen, PA: Schiffer Publishing, 2006.

Silver, Murray. *Behind the Moss Curtain and Other Great Savannah Stories*. Savannah, GA: Bonaventure Books, 2002.

Stavely, John F. *Ghosts and Gravestones of Savannah, Georgia*. Savannah, GA: Historic Tours of America, 2006.

Windham, Kathryn Tucker. *13 Georgia Ghosts and Jeffrey*. Tuscaloosa: University of Alabama Press, 1973.

INTERNET ARTICLES

ABC News. "Man with Amnesia Finds His Family after Searching for 11 Years." abcnews.go.com/Health/man-amnesia-finds/family-searching-11-years/story?id=33864237.

Accgov.com. "Ware-Lyndon Historic House." accgov.com/facilities/facility/Details/29.

Activerain. "Fairy Crosses Found in Fannin County." activerain.com/blogsview/1698055/fairy-crosses-found-in-fannin-county.

American Hauntings. "The Atlanta Ripper: Unsolved American Murders." troytaylor books.blogspot.com/2014/01/the-atlanta-ripper-unsolved-american.html.

Atlas Obscura. "Colonial Park Cemetery." www.atlasobscura.com/places/colonial-park-cemetery-2.

———. "Georgia Guidestones." www.atlasobscura.com/places/georgia-guidestones.

———. "St. James Episcopal Cemetery." www.atlasobscura.com/places/st-james-episcopal-cemetery.

Baxter, Jenn. "The Last Night Out: What Happened to Justin Gaines?" Medium. medium.com/@jennbaxter_69070/the-last-night-out-what-happened-to-justin-gaines-a25e9917f77d.

Brenau University. "Brenau University: Our Story." online.brenau.edu/ourstory/?source_code=GOOGLE7source_campaign_id=5938&utm_campaign_id=3499293168agid=264-83383396&search_keyword=brenau.

———. "The Ghostess with the Mostest." window.brenau.edu/articles/the-ghostess-with-the-mostest.

Chattooga Conservancy. "The Tallulah Gorge." chattoogariver.org/the-tallulah-gorge.

Chicken Fat. "Visiting St. James Episcopal Cemetery in Marietta." Ethunter1.blogspot.com/2012/01/visiting-at-james-episcopal-cemetery-in.html.

City of Griffin. "John Henry 'Doc' Holliday." www.cityofgriffin.com/Home/History/DocHolliday.aspx.

COBB Travel & Tourism. "8 Spooky Spots to Get in the Halloween Spirit." travelcobb.org/8-spooky-spots-halloween-spirit.

Columbus, GA Now. "Haunted Columbus Series: The Talbot County Werewolf Girl." chattvoice.com/haunted-columbus-series-the-talbot-county-werewolf-girl-p2113-142.htm.

Creative Loafing. "Paranormal Activity at the Wren's Nest?" creativeloafing.com/content-462969-paranormal-activity-at-the-wren-s.

Dale J. Young. "The Haunted Fields of Andersonville." dalejyoung.com/the-haunted-fields-of-andersonville.

11Alive News. "Ghostly Image Captured at Marietta Museum." www.11alive.com/article/news/ghostly-image-captured-at-marietta-museum/85-102.

———. "Human Remains Found Near Lake Lanier Raise Hopes for Justin Gaines' Mother." www.11alive.com/article/news/crime/justinpgaines-human-remains/85-908be5f30-4885-8c24-554b9b228e1e#:`:text=12.

———. "It Looks Like Dippin' Dots Falling from the Sky." www.11alive.com/article/weather/graupel-sleet-across/85-532087b-01fa-4d1e82a-03d4265a1.

Explore Georgia. "Bulloch Hall." exploregeorgia.org/roswell/history-heritage/civil-war/bulloch-hall.

———. "The River Nobody Knows: Discovering Georgia's Altamaha." exploregeorgia.org/article/the-river-nobody-knows-discovering-georgias-altamaha-river.

———. "Roswell Mill Ruins in Old Mill Park." exploregeorgia.org/roswell/history-heritage/civil-war/roswell-mill-ruins-in-old-mill-park.

Explore Southern History. "Altamaha-ha: Sea Monster of the Georgia Coast." www.exploresouthernhistory.com/altamahaha.html.

———. "Ghosts of Jekyll Island, Georgia." exploresouthernhistory.com/jekyllghosts.html.

———. "Haunted St. Simons Lighthouse: St. Simons Island, Georgia." www.exploresouthernhistory.com/gastsimons2.html.

Fox5 Atlanta. "Mystery: Ice Falls through Georgia Home." www.fox5atlanta.com/news/mystery-ice-falls-through-georgia-home.

Fright Find. "The Haunted University of Georgia." frightfind.com/university-of-georgia.

Gainesville [GA] Times. "Gainesville Ghosts: The Legend of Agnes." www.gainesvilletimes.com/life/people/gainesville-ghosts-legend-agnes.

Gallivanter Tours. "Little Gracie, Bonaventure's Most Visited Gravesite." gallivantertours.com/savannah/historic-cemteries/Bonaventure-cemetery/little-gracie.

Garden & Gun. "The South's Own Loch Ness Monster?" gardenandgun.com/aarticles/souths-loch-ness-monster.

Georgia College. "Our Heritage & History." gsu.edu/about/history.

Georgia Encyclopedia. "Deportation of Roswell Mill Women." georgiaencyclopedia.org/articles/history-archaeology/deportation-roswell-mill-women.

Georgia Haunted Houses. "Georgia College: Old Governor's Mansion." georgiahauntedhouses.com/real-haunt/Georgia-college-old-governors-mansion.html.

———. "Johnston-Felton-Hay House: Real Haunts in Macon GA." www.georgiahauntedhouses.com/real-haunt/johnstonfeltonhay-house.html.

———. "Kennesaw Mountain National Battlefield Park: Real Haunts in Kennesaw GA." www.georgiahauntedhouses.com/real-haunt/kennesaw-mountain-national-battlefield-park.html.

Georgia Paranormal Society. "The Callaway Plantation." Youtube.com/watch?v=RehuuNN9WO

Ghost City Tours. "The Ghost of Little Gracie Watson." ghostcitytours.com/savannah/ghost-stories/little-gracie.

———. "The Ghosts of Colonial Park Cemetery." ghostcitytours.com/savannah/haunted-places/colonial-park-cemetery.

———. "The Ghosts of the Andrew Low House." ghostcitytours.com/savannah/haunted-places/haunted-houses/andrew-low-house.

———. "The Ghosts of the Hampton Lillibridge House." ghostcitytours.com/savannah/haunted-places/haunted-houses/hampton-lillibridge-house.

———. "The Ghosts of the Kehoe House." ghostcitytours.com/savannah/haunted-places/haunted-hotels/kehoe-house.

———. "The Ghosts of the Marshall House Hotel." ghostcitytours.com/savannah/haunted-places/haunted-hotels/marshall-house-hotel.

———. "Ghosts of the Moon River Brewing Company." ghostcitytours.com/savannah/haunted-places/haunted-restaurants/moon-river-brewing-company.

———. "The Ghosts of the Pink House Restaurant." ghostcitytours.com/savannah/haunted-places/haunted-restaurants/pink-house-restaurant.

———. "The Ghosts of the Pirate's House Restaurant." ghostcitytours.com/savannah/haunted-places/haunted-restaurants/pirates-house.

———. "The Ghosts of Wright Square." ghostcitytours.com/savannah/haunted-places/haunted-savannah-squares/wright-square.

Ghost Savannah. "Ghosts at the Davenport House in Savannah GA?" www.ghostsavannah.com/2014/10/davenport-house-in-savannah.

Ghosts of Georgia. "The Morton Theatre." ghostsofgeorgia.com/Morton-theater-athens-ga-10-11-14.

Go Covington. "Homegrown Trilogy: Orna Villa Haunting in Newton County." govington.com/Blog/homegrown-trilogy-orna-villa-haunting-in-newton-county.

Haunted Houses. "Fort Pulaski." hauntedhouses.com/Georgia/fort-pulaski.

———. "Pirate's House." hauntedhouses.com/Georgia/pirates-house.

Haunted Journeys. "Barnsley Gardens Resort." www.hauntedjourneys.com/haunted-inns/1787-barnsley-gardens-resort.

The Haunted Librarian. "Marietta's First Druggist." thehauntedlibrarian.com/2013/10/13/mariettas-first-druggist.

Haunted Marietta. "The Kennesaw House." www.marietta.com/haunted-places-in-marietta-ga-the-kennesaw-house.

Haunted Rooms. "The Ghosts of Berry College." hauntedrooms.com/Georgia/haunted-places/berry-college-college-mount-berry.

———. "7 Most Haunted Places Augusta GA." www.hauntedrooms.com/Georgia/augusta/haunted-places.

Haunted Savannah Tours. "Ghost of the Owens-Thomas House." hauntedsavannahtours.com/ghost-owens-thomas-house.

The Hauntings of America. "The Most Haunted House in Savannah." hauntsofamerica.blogspot.com/2011/04/most-haunted-house-in-savannah.html.

Haunt World. "About Andersonville Prison." www.hauntworld.com/haunted-hospital-in-andersonville-georgia-andersonville-prison-in-andersonville-georgia.

Hay House Macon. "Historic Home." www.hayhousemacon.org/history/historic-home.

Headstuff. "Anjette Lyles, Restaurateur of Death." www.headstuff.org/culture/history/anjette-lyles-restaurateur-death-poison.

Her Campus. "Ghost Stories of Savannah " www.hercampus.com/school/scad/ghost-stories-savannah.

———. "SCAD Haunted Housing." www.hercampus.com/school/scad/scad-haunted-housing.

Historic Hotels of America. "Jekyll Island Club Resort." historichotels.org/us/hotels-resorts/jekyll-island-club-resort/ghost-stories.php.

History Atlanta. "The Wren's Nest." historyatlanta.com/the-wren's-nest.

History. "Doc Holliday Dies of Tuberculosis." www.history.com/this-day-in-history/doc-holliday-dies-of-tuberculosis.

———. "Jimmy Carter Files Report on UFO Sighting." www.history.com/this-day-in-history/carter-files-report-on-ufo-sighting.

History Net. "Explore the Haunting Remnants of Civil War Prisons." www.historynet.com/explore-the-haunting-remains-of-civil-war-prisons.htm.

History Southeast. "The Ghost of the St. Simon Lighthouse." historysoutheast.com/stsimons2.

Inspirock. "Callaway Plantation, Washington." www.inspirock.com/united-states/washington-georgia/callaway-plantation-a420378299.

In the Know. "Georgia's Lake Lanier Is 100 Percent Haunted." www.intheknow.com/post/lake-lanier-georgia.

Into the Wonder. "Uncanny Georgia: The Wog." intothewonder.wordpress.com/2-15/07/17/uncanny-georgia-the-wog.

Jamie Davis Writes. "Ghosts." Jamiedaviswrites.com/tag/ghosts/page/4.

Just History. "The Lost Confederate Treasury." www.historynaked.com/lost-confederate-treasury.

The Kehoe House. "The Kehoe House History." www.kehoehouse.com/haunted.htm.

Legends of America. "Confederate Gold in Wilkes County, Georgia." www.legendsofamerica.com/confederate-gold-georgia.

————. "Legends of Fort Mountain, Georgia." www.legendsofamerica.com/ga-fortmountain.

The Lineup. "The Creepy Halloween Legend of Mary Meinert's Grave." the-line-up.com/mary-meinert.

————. "The Spooky Ruins of Georgia's Central State Hospital." the-line-up.com/central-state-hospital-georgia.

LiveJournal. "Tallulah Gorge Legends." care-you-now.livejournal.com/2071.html.

Lowndes County Historical Society Museum. "Doc Holliday." valdostamuseum.com/exhibitions/online-exhibits-2/people/doc-holliday.

Mary Hallberg. "The Dark History of Georgia's Central Hospital." www.maryhallbergmedia.com/post/the-dark-history-of-georgia-s-central-state-hospital.

Military Ghosts. "Fort Pulaski: The Commander's Spirit." militaryghosts.com/Pulaski.html.

The Moonlit Road. "The Dinner Party: Savannah Bonaventure Dinner Party: Ghost Story." themoonlitroad.com/savannah-bonaventure-cemetery-ghost-story.

Moon River Brewing Company. "A Haunted History." https://www.moonriverbrewing.com/the-ghosts

Morton Theatre. "Morton Theatre." mortontheatre.com/history.

Mule Day Southern Heritage Festival. "Welcome to Callaway Plantation." Muledaysouthernheritagefestival.org/about-callaway-plantation.

Murderpedia. "Anjette Donovan Lyles." murderpedia.org/female.L/l/lyles-anjette.htm.

Mysterious Trip. "Kehoe House." mysterioustrip.com/kehoe-house-savannah-haunted-story.

National Cemetery Administration. "Marietta National Cemetery." cem.va.gov/cems/nchp/Marietta.asp.

National Park Service. "Augusta Cotton Exchange Building." nps.gov/nr/travel/augusta/augustacottonex.html.

———. "Battle of Kolb's Farm." nps.gov/hps/abpp/battles/ga014.htm.

National Register of Historic Places. "Johnston-Hay House." nrhp.focus.nps.gov/atregsearchresult.do?fullresult=true&recordid=27.

Nchschant.com. "Urban Legends from Marietta, Kennesaw, and Roswell Explored." nchschant.com/1847/investigative/urban-legends-from-marietta-kennesaw-and-roswell-explored.

New Georgia Encyclopedia. "Confederate Gold." www.georgiaencyclopedia.org/articles/history-archaeology/confederate-gold.

———. "Georgia Guidestones." www.georgiaencyclopedia.org/articles/history-archaeology/georgia-guidestones.

———. "The Georgia Wonder." www.georgiaencyclopedia.org/articles/arts-culture/georgia-wonder-phenomenon.

News West 9. "Is a Real Ghost Haunting a Civil War Battlefield in Georgia?" www.newswest9.com/article/news/is-a-real-ghost-haunting-a-civil-war-battlefield-in-georgia/513-c4059b50-ba55-44cd-9517-b35e85833414.

Nightly Spirits. "The Ghost of Gracie Watson." nightlyspirits.com/the-ghost-of-gracie-watson.

———. "The Haunted Colonial Park Cemetery in Savannah." nightlyspirits.com/the-haunted-colonial-park-cemetery-in-savannah.

———. "The Haunted Moon River Brewing Company in Savannah." nightlyspirits.com/the-haunted-moon-river-brewing-company-savannah.

Oconee Hill Cemetery. "Oconee Hill Cemetery." Oconeehillcemetery.com.

Only in Your State. "These 10 Haunted Cemeteries Are Not for the Faint of Heart." www.onlyinyourstate.com/georgia/haunted-cemeteries-in-ga.

———. "The Story behind This Ghost Town Cemetery in Georgia Will Chill You to the Bone." www.onlyinyourstate.com/georgia/story-ghost-town-cemetery-ga.

Paranormal Daily News. "Echoes of Civil War's Past." paranormaldailynews.com/haunted-roswell-mill/3783.

The Pirate's House. "The Pirate's House: History." thepirateshouse.com.

R. Armstrong @ Augusta U. "Hauntings on Campus." rajarmstrong.com/projects/Summerville/hauntings-on-campus.

The Red and Black. "Ghosts of the Classic City: The Morton Theatre's Haunted Phenomena." redandblack.com/culture/ghosts-of-the-classic-city-the-morton-theatre-s-haunted-phenomena/article_62d98990-e763-11e9-a08d-ffcd616b5c47.html.

———. "Ghosts of the Classic City: Who Is the Ghost Inside the Lyndon House?" www.redandblack.com/culture/ghosts-of-the-classic-city-who-is-the-ghost-inside-the-lyndon-house/article_11e30f9a-ec98-11e9-b3f4-5ba195d8682f.html.

————. "Haunted Halls of UGA: Spookiest Spots on Campus." www.redandblack.com/culture/the-haunted-halls-of-uga-spookiest-spots-on-campus/article_af61fec0-d727-11e8-9608-bb1bcb546196.htm.

————. "Sorority House Haunted by Heartbroken Bride." www.redandblack.com/variety/sorority-house-haunted-by-heartbroken-bride/article_cd32daf8-77b0-5e87-a21e-167a2c39d8d3.html.

Roadside America. "Expedition Bigfoot, the Sasquatch Museum." www.roadsideamerica.com.

Road Trippers. "Orna Villa." maps.roadtrippers.com/us/oxford-ga/points-of-interest/orna-villa.

Salty Waves Spanish Moss. "Walking with a Ghost in Fort Pulaski." saltywavesspanishmoss.com/2020/09/30/walking-with-a-ghost-at-fort-pulaski.

SCAD District. "Exploring Architectural History: The Haunted House You Never Dreamed Of." scaddistrict.com/2021/05/18/exploring-architectural-history-the-haunted-house-you.

Seeks Ghosts. "Battle of Kennesaw Mountain." seeksghosts.blogspot.com/2015/06/battle-of-kennesaw-mountain.html.

Society of Architectural Historians. "Sibley Mill." sah-archipedia.org/buildings/GA-01-245-0029.

Southern Flavors Savannah. "The Hampton Lillibridge House." southernflavorssavannah.com/2020/04/08/the-hampton-lillibridge-house.

Southern Gothic Media. "The Curse of Lake Lanier." Southerngothicmedia.com/lake-lanier.

Southern Spirit Guide. "Davenport House." www.southernspiritguide.org/guests-and-ghosts-on-columbia-square.

————. "Ghosts of Athens and the University of Georgia." www.southernspiritguide.org/town-and-gown-ghosts-of-athens-and-the-university-of-georgia.

————. "Kennesaw Mountain National Battle Park." www.southernspiritguide.org/kennesaw-mountain-battlefield-experiences-georgia.

————. "Revisiting Ezekiel Harris: The Ezekiel Harris House, Augusta, Georgia." www.southernspiritguide.org/revisiting-ezekiel-harris-the-ezekiel-harris-house-augusta-georgia.

The Stoddard Firm. "Lake Lanier Isn't Haunted, but It's Definitely Unsafe." thestoddardfirm.com/lake-lanier-unsafe.

13wmaz.com. "Hard to Imagine Anyone Killing People that They Were Supposed to Love." www.13wmaz.com/article/news/history/anjette-lyles-macon-serial-killer-crimeinve.

————. "Just Curious: What Is the History of the Hay House?" www.13wmaz.com/article/news/local/just-curious-what-is-the-history-of-the-hay-house/93-523729061.

Works Cited

Union Recorder. "Dixie Haygood a Haunting Part of Local History." www.unionrecorder.com/news/lifestyles/dixie-haygood-a-haunting-part-of-local-history/article_be894003-8cc5-56c3-a90e-1d060020ddbe.html.

Valdosta Today. "The Legend of Crystal Lake." valdostatoday.com/living/2019/09/the-legend-of-crystal-lake.

Vanishing South Georgia. "Crystal Lake, Irwin County." vanishingsouthgeorgia.com/2014/04/10/crystal-lake-irwin-county-2.

Viking Fusion. "Calling All Spirits: The Chilling Stories of Campus Ghosts." vikingfusion.com/2019/10/31/calling-all-spirits-the-chilling-stories-of-campus-ghosts.

Visit Athens GA. "Haunted Athens: A Guide to Athens GA's Spookiest Destinations." www.visitathensga.com/blog/post/haunted-athens-a-guide-to-athens-spookiest-destinations.

Visit Milledgeville. "The Little Georgia Magnet: The Legend of Milledgeville's Magical Resident, Dixie Haygood." www.visitmilledgeville.org/blog/post/the-little-georgia-magnet-the-legend-of-milledgevilles-magical-resident-dixie-haygood.

———. "Memory Hill Cemetery Haunted Stories." www.visitmilledgeville.org/blog/post/memory-hill-cemetery-haunted-stories.

Visit Savannah. "Owens-Thomas House & Slave Quarters." www.visitsavannah.com/profile/owens-thomas-house-slave-quarters/5601.

———. "Telfair Museums." www.visitsavannah.com.

Wander North Georgia. "Everything You Wanted to Know about Bigfoot in North Georgia." wandernorthgeorgia.com/north-georgia-bigfoot.

———. "The Story of the Sautee Nacoochee Indian Mound." wandernorthgeorgia.com/the-story-of-the-sautee-nacoochee-indian-mound.

Waymarking. "Wright Square: Savannah, GA: Ghosts and Hauntings." www.waymarking.com/waymarks/wm3Z3M_Wright_Square_Savannah_GA.

Wbko.com. "Possible Bigfoot Sightings Reported in Northeast Georgia, According to Facebook Page." wbko.com/content/news/Possible-Bigfoot-sightings-reported-in-northeast-Georgia-according-to-Facebook-page-510491451.html.

Werewolf Page. "The Talbot County Werewolf." www.werewolfpage.com/myths/talbot.htm.

Werewolves. "The Werewolf Girl of Georgia." www.werewolves.com/the-werewolf-girl-of-georgia.

Winters Media. "The History: Remembering Mayhayley Lancaster." www.wintersmedia.net.

Wtvm.com. "Is There Bigfoot in Georgia?" www.wtvm.com/story/4906451/is-there-bigfoot-in-georgia.

X-Project Paranormal Magazine. "More Haunted Colleges." www.xprojectmagazine.com/archives/paranormal/hc_html.

Zme Science. "Georgia Guidestones: Mysterious Instructions for the Post Apocalypse." /www.zmescience.com/other/feature-post/georgia-guidestones-mysterious-instructions-for-the-post-apocalypse.

JOURNALS AND MAGAZINES

Eury, Perry. "Stone Pile Gap and a Fountain of Youth." *Smoky Mountain Living Magazine*, August 1, 2017.

Wolfe, Matt. "The Last Unknown Man." *The New Republic*. newrepublic.com/article/138068/last-unknown-man.

NEWSPAPER ARTICLES

Corley, Laura. "A Witch? A Ghost? Who Was Dixie Haygood, a Milledgeville Legend from the Late 1880s?" *Macon Telegraph*, July 19, 2019.

Fabian, Liz. "Haunted Hay House? Photographer Wonders If He Caught Ghost on Camera." *Macon Telegraph*, October 31, 2010.

Hoover, Marc. "Marc Hoover: The Atlanta Ripper." *Clermont Sun*, June 3, 2021.

Hudak, Stephen. "No-Man's Land: Amnesia Stole His Identity for 11 Years." *Orlando Sentinel*, September 22, 2015.

Mirshak, Meg. "Ghostly Hauntings Reported at Augusta Sites." *Augusta Chronicle*, October 30, 2011.

News Observer. "Man Reports Seeing 7–8 Foot Tall Creature Walking across Rural Road in Georgia." May 28, 2019.

Obrien, Cailin. "Officials Still Hope to ID Skeletal Remains Found in Buford Two Years Ago." *Gwinnett Daily Post*, February 22, 2017.

Oliver, Kristen. "Some Say Ghost Haunts Pearce Auditorium at Brenau University." *Gainesville Times*, October 27, 2016.

Silvey, Hailey. "Campus Hauntings." *Enotah Echoes*, October 27, 2010.

Thornton, Carolyn. "The Spirits of Savannah." *Sun-Sentinel*, October 13, 1991.

Vardeman, Johnny. "Native American Legends Change over the Years." *Gainesville Times*, January 7, 2022.

Walker, Pam. "The Folklore and Legends of Barnsley Gardens." *Calhoun Times*, October 16, 2020.

Willetts, Mitchelol. "'Graupel' Is Falling from the Sky over Parts of Georgia—but What Is It?" *Telegraph*, January 13, 2021.

ABOUT THE AUTHOR

D r. Alan Brown is a professor of English and folklore at the University of West Alabama. As a member of the Alabama Humanities Alliance, Dr. Brown has been presenting public programs on southern folklore and literature since 1994. He also presents ghost walks of Livingston, Alabama, and the University of West Alabama several times a year. Dr. Brown has published over forty books on ghostlore, including *Eerie Alabama* (2019), *Legends and Lore of Mississippi* (2020) and *Kentucky Legends and Lore* (2021). Every year, Dr. Brown and his wife, Marilyn, travel through the South in search of material for his books. When Dr. Brown is not teaching or writing, he enjoys reading thrillers, watching old movies and playing with his two grandsons, Cade and Owen Walker, and with Holly, his Maltese.

Visit us at
www.historypress.com